Gerhard Tersteegen

Focusing Within

Gozalov Books
The Hague

ISBN: 9789079889723; 978-90-79889-72-3

Editors: Convent of the Mother of God Portaïtissa, Trazegnies, Belgium, portaitissa@skynet.be
Joya Stevenson, Book Editing Associates, Philadelphia, PA, USA, joyaeditor@yahoo.com (Letters 34, 35, 36, 39)

Translators: Guram Kochi and Marijcke Tooneman
Design: Guram Kochi and Marijcke Tooneman
Cover image: Tatiana Spasolomskaya, spas1725@mail.ru
The Scriptural quotes are taken from the The Sacred Bible, Catholic Public Domain Version with thanks to the http://www.sacredbible.org/catholic/index.htm
Footnotes: Hegoumen Peter (Mescherinov), igpetr@yandex.ru

© Gozalov Books, The Hague, 2023
Tel.: 00 31 (0) 70 352 15 65
E-mail: gozalovbooks@planet.nl
Website: www.hetsmallepad.nl

TABLE OF CONTENTS

This book contains a small selection of the letters of the German Protestant mystic and poet Gerhard Tersteegen (1697 - 1769) to his followers. Tersteegen was a representative of the pietism movement, or rather, one of its directions, the so-called "quiet in the land", according to the psalmist: "For they speak not peace: but they devise deceitful matters against them that are quiet in the land." (Ps. 35:20, KJV)

In the book "Great Saints" by Walter Nigg, Associate Professor at the University of Zurich (Plugsma Publishers, Amsterdam, 1958), Tersteegen is called "a saint of Protestantism" and is ranked among such great saints as Francis of Assisi, Joan of Arc, Teresa of Avila and John of the Cross.

The letters are selected on the following topics, which are vital to every Christian:

I.   Overview of the inner Christian Life
II.   On the receptive Acceptance of the Grace of God
III.   On Prayer and Inner Work
IV.   About God's Peace
V.   About the Childlikeness in Christ
VI.   On the Struggle against Sin. Spiritual Warfare
VII.   On the Cross and Suffering
VIII.   About the Life of God in us
IX.   On the Church and Church Life

Tersteegen offers a way of direct appeal to God, through the Lord Jesus Christ. He explains what are the rules and stages of this way and how a Christian can follow it in his everyday life, even without changing anything outwardly. The main thing on this way is a passive, "accepting" attitude in the matter of saving the soul: namely, salvation comes only from

God, not from the person himself, and you need to learn not to hinder God's work of saving you. These tips can especially help those who have already experienced spiritual insights and pray God to give them to them daily: "Give us this day our life-sustaining bread." (Mt. 6:11).

The given English translation is from the Russian translation of selected letters of Tersteegen, made from the German original by Hegoumen Peter (Meshcherinov), head of the homestead of the Danilovsky monastery in Domodedovo. Hegoumen Peter translated and published the writings of several German Protestant mystics, having found that their experiences and teachings open a way out of the inner impasse in which many Orthodox and Catholic Christians find themselves. Namely, after many years of regular prayers, confession, communion, ascetic practices, they still cannot experience a living communion with God, and, disappointed, abandon the church, and often, lose their faith in God. Here is what Hegoumen Peter writes about this phenomenon: "All this is a kind of "asceticism of self-willed action", a person acts from himself, on his own; God, as it were, is "bracketed", and the whole life of a Christian turns into observing his sins, fear of sins, etc. Such a "vicious circle" of current Orthodox-ascetic pedagogy is one of the main reasons why man, though observing all the prescriptions of the Church tradition, does not find God and abandons the church."

Tersteegen's direct way, which seems very simple, however, has its own "boundary conditions".

Here is what Hegoumen Peter says about this: "Tersteegen speaks of a living communion with God, of how to "taste and see" the goodness of God (Ps. 34:9). Some listeners get the impression that when I talk about Tersteegen's teachings, I am "criticizing Orthodoxy". But that's not the case at all. My attention is directed exclusively to the established "grassroots" pastoral-church pedagogy. I criticize not the dogmatic and moral teaching of the Church at all, but the failure of the aforementioned pastoral-church pedagogy: Christians are "stuck" at the initial stage of the Christian way, since information about further stages and methods of their achievement are not communicated to them, due to the absence of such knowledge among the priests themselves.

On the other hand, as it became clear to me from experience, a considerable number of my interlocutors have not yet reached even the initial stage of the Christian way, while their demands and claims are very high. It very often happens that people get involved in discussions about elevated matters, about Christian communion with God, about its possibility or impossibility, and complain that they "do not succeed", that "God did not predestine us"; they criticize the topics we raise, and so on, but just dig even deeper, and it turns out that they do not understand and do not observe even elementary rules of the spiritual path. Their ethics is completely distorted. They are full of powerful addictions. Their social relations are distorted. The mental health of some requires treatment... And they are completely unaware of all this but still want to communicate with God.

But all should be done in a proper way: first of all a person must sort out his inner and outer circumstances and learn the basic Christian moral and spiritual teachings and practices, including repentance, confession, improving life, the ability to ascetically observe oneself, the ability to receive help through the Sacraments and through other church activities, etc. Then it will become clear what hinders communion with God in each specific case, and then a lot of things will become clear for the person which, to put it simply, will bring him/her to their senses.

Hence: Tersteegen's instructions are addressed to Christians, in relation to whom a certain presumption is valid by default. Namely, these people want to be *true* Christians and make

every effort to achieve this. From what I say, sometimes one may get the impression that nothing needs to be done at all, and that every person can easily "taste and see" (Ps. 35:9). No, you have to do the work, as the Kingdom of Heaven is taken by force (Mt.11:12), and not all people, but only those pure in heart will see God (Mt.5:8). (Being "pure in heart" in a real life process, and not in abstractions and not in their own imagination, of course.)
So the presumption is:
- Church traditional faith;
- The regular reading and meditating of the Holy Scripture;
- Being rooted in the church (in the "good" sense of the word);
- clashes with the limitations of the church sphere, which force a Christian to look for the means to move further along the Christian way: those clashes will come by themselves;
- And most importantly, practicing evangelical ethics in life and a sober and humble view of oneself.
This is what a Christian needs to "do", and apply all his/her efforts here."

Hegoumen Peter is one of the signatories of the appeal of a small group of the clergy of the Russian Orthodox Church in March 2022 calling for reconciliation and the end to the war in Ukraine.
https://docs.google.com/forms/d/e/1FAIpQLSca_U5DOLd-Kykv5VZFuJkyMf04gAArOEhYDRDXNHVso1YGrmQ/view-form

Guram Kochi and Marijcke Tooneman

The Hague, May 2023

I. Overview of the inner Christian Life

LETTER 1. ABOUT THE THREEFOLD BIRTH OF A CHRISTIAN

Beloved brother in the Lord Jesus!

The fact that so many brothers and sisters at your place and in other places are so worried about my life in the suffering flesh and its prolongation, truly fills me with great humility. Their heartfelt attitude consoles and encourages me. May the divine love reward them for this a hundredfold!
Looking through the calendar of my life, I find many red-marked and black-marked days there. I call the black marks my many sins, infirmities, foolishness and all kinds of flaws, which are bigger than those who love me can imagine. Even up to this day this deficiency rather saddens me. However, it does not drive me to the point of depression and despair. The red-marked days draw my attention much more strongly. In those days I experienced the abounding grace and the power of the scarlet blood of my Lord Jesus Christ. May He preserve and increase the precious working of His grace in me and in all hearts, which, by His benevolence, are connected to my heart through love. So that we may live worthily (Philippians 1:27) not only for God, Who redeemed and called us (1 Thess. 2:12), but also for one another, to His children according to His grace (Eph. 4:1), and that none of us would be late (Heb. 4:1), but all of us could, in joy and jubilation, celebrate together with Angels and saints our last birthday!

For the children of God have three birthdays. In the first birth, by nature, they pass from the cramped dungeon of the mother's womb into the light of this earthly world. Then the child cries (ah! Not in vain!) while the family rejoices.

In their second, the blessed birth, the birth anew (John 3:3) Christians are being led step by step out of the cramped and dark state of fallen nature into the light of grace. Then the child of God that is born, mostly weeps and grieves; but the angels in heaven rejoice over him, as they rejoice when they see at least one sinner who is repentant (Luke 15:10).
What we call death, the first Christians called and celebrated as the birthday of martyrs and saints.

This third birth, the death of the body, frees God's children from the bonds of this world and frees them from the tight imprisonment of the body of death (Rom. 7:24) and from every burden and anxiety, when the soul is born to the true joy and passes into the vastness of the sweetest sorrowless eternity. This last birth is often painful and unsightly, so that the child of grace suffers extremely, groans and cries, while passing through it, but all this is for his good.

For sooner or later everything comes to an end, and the soul cries out together with Jesus: "It is consummated." (John 19:30). Angels as God's encampments (Gen. 32:2), are ready to receive a child, born into blissful eternity, onto their hands and carry him as a Lazarus into the bosom of Abraham, that is, God's bosom (Luke 16:22). Then they rejoice child-like heartily, that a Christian was born in the world of light, love and joy. His true birthday is celebrated; then all heaven sings a hymn to the God of love, and the angels add to each verse: "Amen! Glory to God in the highest! Hallelujah!" And knowing this, it is proper for us to go on, bold in the Lord and trusting in Him, not being afraid of brief birth pangs (that is, numer-ous hardships of our fleeting earthly wandering), but wholly entrusting ourselves to God and submitting to Him. We know that our labor "is not useless in the Lord." (1 Cor.15:58) Amen!

Lord Jesus, "Remain with us, because it is toward evening and now daylight is declining." (Luke 24:29)

My heart blesses all and each of you.
May the Lord Jesus seal this with His blessing!
Amen.

In Christ Jesus, our blessed Saviour, honored sister!

I have more than once intended to write you a few lines; however, since I do not know you personally and I do not know the disposition of your soul, I've been postponing those intentions. But from time to time I remembered you in my feeble prayers. First of all, I thanked God and I never cease to give thanks for the fact that He, by His great grace, began to enlighten your eyes, so that you could understand the sinful flaw of man, the insignificance of this world and the importance of eternal matters. Also I thanked Him for giving you desire and aspiration, which, I hope, you cherish sincerely, to become truly healed of your sins, renounce vanity, and live pleasing the Lord. If you, beloved sister, find in yourself such a disposition of the heart, then consider yourself much obliged to give, together with me, thanks to God for this. For the slightest action of God's grace is incomparably more precious than anything this world can give us.

The first step on the path of godliness is a change of the direction of our lives from eternal perdition to eternal salvation. I'm asking you to think more often about this before God. What is not kept in mind is easily lost. What would satan and the fallen world not give for us to reverse our mindset! May the Lord keep you , me and all of His children from this. Therefore I, thanking Him for you, also pray to Him that He will not allow the enemy to confuse you and turn you away from God or immerse you in spiritual sleep and carelessness.

Oh! Many I knew who had a good start, but after a while they again turned their ears to this world and to the fallen reason, gave up and lost heart! Other ones, though not entirely looking back (Luke 9:62), stopped at the initial beneficial actions and changes and did not advance to the entire new birth (John 3:3) and inner union with God. Third ones, when they wanted to continue the spiritual life, a particularly great grace of God was needed, so that they may be shown the true way. For they always strayed and came on the path of stumbling, errors and delusions... I'm not saying this to drive you into despondency, but to encourage you to pursue incessant prayer (1 Thess. 5:17), extreme caution (Eph. 5:15), and great seriousness. (Philippians 2:12).

If you, dear sister, ask me what do I consider as the true spiritual path, then I will answer you in general: this way is the one that the Lord Jesus heralds us in the Gospel when He says: "If anyone is willing to come after me, let him deny himself, and take up his cross, and follow me." (Matthew 16:24). Here we see three commandments; if we add to each of them incessant prayer (Luke 18:1), then in these four commandments the entire true Christianity will be contained; and neither fallen reason, nor this world will be able to contradict them. May the Lord Jesus, Who spoke them, grant you always to understand and perform them according to your position and condition!

For a better understanding of this, let me suggest to you some simple guidance. Imagine that our beloved Saviour says to you now and every day: "Deny yourself in what you find in yourself. E.g. you've noticed love, joy, hope inside you in relation to something created, outside of God; you've become aware of how your pride and self-pleasing manifests itself in something, even in spiritual matters: deny yourself. Do not follow the attraction of your own thoughts, feelings and de-

sires which come from your fallen nature, but act in a holy way in deeds and words, in pursuits and when resting, in food and drink, etc., opposing your godless ego (of course, avoiding extremes and harm to health).
Pray incessantly for blessing, wisdom, courage, patience and strength and take up your cross.

You needn't design your cross yourself, but just accept the one that is already offered to you. The cross from this world, when it despises, ridicules, hates, tortures and persecutes you. The cross from satan, when it torments you through temptations, evil thoughts and hypnotic delusions.

The cross from God and His providence, which lets you undergo sorrows, illnesses, countless misfortunes and spiritual ordeals, as e.g. when He would conceal and withdraw from your awareness His strength and grace, and the like. The cross from yourself, that is the weakness of your bodily composition, illnesses, a feeling of spiritual weakness, inconstancy and volatility, and, even the sins that you commit against your will or by recklessness. All this is your cross; take it upon yourself. Taking it means to frame your mind in such a way that you will have very few carefree days on this earth.
Be strong and be patient; and pray incessantly for courage, patience and strength, and follow Me. Commit yourself to Me with all hope. Surrender your will completely into My hands. Become like a little child who cannot walk by himself and doesn't know where he should go. Close the eyes of the fallen reason and hold on to Me by faith. Pay attention to the movements of My Spirit inside you; and just as I convince, admonish and draw you, so follow Me in simplicity, not worrying about anything (Phil. :6). I Myself have traveled this road of self-denial and the cross and I will guide you unerringly through it. I know best what is useful for you, just hold on to

Me; do not take your eyes off Me. And just as I have preceded you and continue preceding you inwardly and outwardly, so follow Me, at the same time praying incessantly for faith, simplicity and fidelity.

I emphasize again, beloved sister, that prayer is necessary for all our spiritual work. Partly because we are poor and weak on our own, having nothing and being able to do nothing, but unceasingly pray for alms at the gates of the grace of the Lord (Prov. 8:34). Partly because we cannot digest solid food when there is much of it and get disgusted with it, if we are not given milk with it (1 Cor. 3:2). The teachings of the Lord Jesus about the cross and self-denial are for our fallen nature like solid food. Therefore no matter how sincere we were striving for it in the beginning, over time it inevitably becomes indigestible for us and too bitter, unless it softens and becomes sweet through our incessant prayer.

By prayer, I mean not so much asking, desires and aspirations of the soul in order to receive one or another gift from God, but every pursuit of our spirit and our faith regarding God and Divine matters. In Scripture this is called "walking in God's sight" and "His presence at one's right hand" (Gen. 17:1; Ps. 15:8). It is this cornerstone and elevated treasure of true Christianity to which I would like to draw your particular and focused attention, dear sister, for its correct understanding and implementation comprises the entire spiritual life and those commandments of Christ we are talking about. And since I consider walking in God's sight and in His presence being of utmost importance and necessity for me, I wish with all my heart that it would become your only and incessant work too.

I will say a few more words so that you can better understand, what is the prayer, which the Lord Jesus, our Example, and His disciples loved so much and to which they have been so zealously resorting (Luke 6:12; Acts 1:14). Generally speaking, I understand the prayer as the innermost, closest and nearest communication with God. This means that we believe and come to know God as omnipresent, and especially, being present in us. Onto Him, as onto the one Who is present in us, we focus reverently and lovingly our mind and heart as often as possible, (and, if possible, incessantly). This means that we, inwardly prostrating ourselves before Him, worship Him and glorify Him and commit ourselves to Him as His eternal property. We open ourselves to Him and speak lovingly to the Lord as with our most intimate Friend. Faith and love teach us all this .

If we talk about the details of praying this prayer, then in my opinion it is necessary firstly, that as soon as one realizes that he or she, due to external objects and matters, has become diverted from God and from remembering Him, he should focus within.

Secondly (this I would highly recommend especially to you, dear sister), you should schedule some specific period for this focusing within, let it be at least for half an hour or fifteen minutes twice a day. During this time you need to put aside all your pursuits and thoughts about them and put yourself in solitude before God. This not so much for the communication of your needs to Him, but foremost in order to, having focused your scattered thoughts and feelings, turn your mind and heart to contemplation of God and His presence or of any of His Divine property. Reveal completely the depths of your soul to Him and pay heed, silently and speechlessly, whether the Lord would deign to produce in your inner some of His actions or announce something to you. But all this should be performed in simplicity, humility, quietness and rather by heart than by head, since all this must be the work of God's Spirit, not of ourselves. In the beginning it might feel hard and annoying for our nature; but the further the easier, and finally such a prayer becomes the true life and property of the soul. Then the soul, already during the life of the body, is raised up to heaven and is filled with the fullness of God that surpasses all knowledge (Eph. 3:19), which no one can take away from the soul (John 16:22). May the Great God of love grant you, me and thousands of people who seek Him, to experience it in our being!

Behold, beloved sister, what the Lord has given me as the message for you. I pray Him to attach His admonition and grace to the lines of my letter! Greetings to all seekers who fear the Lord known to you, excluding no one.

Beloved brother in Christ!

I received your kind letter through brother N. Your previous messages didn't require my specific answers. I can hardly answer this present letter either, in which you speak of your still continuing a state of spiritual darkness and emptiness. I am feeble and ignorant and not experienced in the ways of the Lord and all I could say to you, you already know beforehand. So I had better take a break with regards to your and my specifics and I will try to elaborate on the general truths of the inner Christian life.

The driving force in our inner damaged, fallen nature, or ego, which turned itself away from God, consists mainly in self-love and self-will. The essence and power of the divine life consists in pure love and total surrender of oneself and all that one is to God. When the life of the ego diminishes, then the divine life, according to the measure of the ego's diminution, increases. A person can be holy in the eyes of people, carrying at the same time the deposits of self-love and willfulness in the depths of his soul and thus being very far from a pure, blessed life. Oh! Where are the Christians who began to hate the life of their ego? (Luke 14:26). And how few are those in whom you can see that they did not love their own lives even unto death! (Rev. 12:11).

When a person turns to God, then he, obeying the guidance of his conscience, takes on to die to sin and to the influences of this world (Rom. 2:6; Col. 2:20). A Christian novice is strict, zealous and indefatigable in appearance and outward activity. He has a lot of power and he resolutely moves forward, for the commanding impulses of grace and the fear of God, on the one hand, and on the other hand, delightful tasting of many gifts of God, which he feels and receives, draw him and as it were, carry his soul. Although it seems to him that it is his soul that does everything by itself and through itself. Such a Christian novice is often a true hero in his intentions and deeds. But the big noise and excessive activity of his power of reason, emotions and body do not allow his soul to become really quiet and immerse in itself. That's why the ontological damage of our fallen nature for the most part remains rooted in the heart. Moreover, our pride inconspicuously and in the most subtle way grows even more, feeding itself on our zeal, virtues and spiritual gifts. Our self-will manifests itself in the condemnation of neighbors and lack of compassion towards them; in hardness and ossification of our opinions, actions and outward works of piety; finally, in constant self-straining, in stubborn self-activity and inability to surrender ourselves to God, even in prayer.

Therefore, we must become aware of the power of life of our ego and uproot it from the soul in some other way.

This occurs partly in an active, partly in a passive (acceptive) way.

Our pride is eradicated in an active way, when it is denied anything that can feed it. A Christian avoids all unnecessary amenities and physical pleasures; he won't do something for which he will be praised and honored if there are no solid reasons for this; he wants to keep a low profile; he seeks to immediately erase from his memory the good that he does; he tries to correlate everything with God; he does not allow his thoughts to enjoy anything that might cause self-pleasing, etc.

Our pride is actively weakened, when we prefer to obey rather than command; when we do not do or say anything that our will wishes excessively, but we try to act contrary to it. However, cutting off our own will applies only to the matters of minor important things (go somewhere, do or say something, read, etc.), the realizing or non-realizing of which cannot cause disruption or harm. However as to the matters which belong to our duties, it is necessary to carry out conscientiously.

However, also in these matters, without sticking to them and without vehemence, so that we would be ready at all times at the slightest sign of God's providence to calmly put them aside. This is the way for a Christian to deal with everything in his/her life. In a nutshell: a Christian must strive both inwardly and in all his actions to be quiet, joyful and humble. If something hard or hostile should arise in his soul, it needs to be immersed in the sweetest element of meekness. And in this way a Christian can, secretly and silently deny himself a thousand times, producing no noise, so that even those with whom we live wouldn't notice it. First of all, it is necessary to watch that the soul would not act rudely, not like a strict observer of the law, intimidating in a harsh way, but peacefully and gently, through God's love and for the sake of this love.

The best and most useful activity, which weakens and uproots our pride and self-will, and which must be the core of the above mentioned, is the inner communion with God in faith and prayer of the heart. For this a Christian can and should find an opportunity to retire from time to time during the day. When the soul places itself in the presence of the Lord in some kind of inner, quiet, child-like and sincere way and gazes at Him in faith, then every temptation soon becomes powerless. God's presence exposes and mortifies the subtlest twists and turns of self-indulgence; the hard and devastating influences of nature and soul will lose their power. Those influences become flexible, soft and meek and thus the soul gradually becomes capable of receiving God's revelations and His sharing Himself with the soul.

All this is sometimes accompanied by much delight, lightness and light, and sometimes by aridity and darkness. But these are side effects and they are not significant, although some might come to the point that their inner sorrow becomes so intensified that they can't follow the above mentioned advice, they do not see what should be done. A good piece of advice is often required.

I see that my letter is getting too long while, I just touched upon the issues of inner aridity, darkness and suffering, with which our pride and self-will are destroyed. There are many kinds of inner darkness and sorrows, according to the states and properties of the soul. For some sorrows and comforts, light and darkness alternate often enough; others have periods of excruciating suffering for a long time. Some sorrows come beforehand in order to guide the soul from the coarse self-willed activity and (I would say) outward piety on the path of inner self-denial and prayer. Many souls cannot withstand these trials of sorrow and either return to the life of this world (2 Pet. 2:20-22), or compel themselves to self-willed piety, where there is no God, and then they often go in circles for their whole life. Some sorrows, alternating, accompany the aforementioned spiritual work; other kind of sorrows, a very deep suffering, follow this work. Some suffering we inflict upon ourselves; some are of God's hand.

How do we know whether our afflictions are God's guidance? It is necessary to examine yourself and find inside yourself the following:

1) fear to displease God;

2) striving for sanctification, that is, for life in God;

3) conviction of the impossibility of helping oneself;

4) one's humble, realistic estimation   of one's spiritual achievements etc.

If the above mentioned is there, then all temptations, trials, spiritual darkness, aridity and all sorts of sorrows and sufferings undoubtedly do not harm us, but serve to weaken and, finally, to completely eradicate our pride and self-will. The peculiarity of these sorrows is that often, instead of zeal for goodness, joy and lightness we feel heaviness, apathy and unwillingness to do anything at all; instead of the gifts of grace we feel darkness, aridity and inability to do anything; instead of virtues we encounter numerous temptations, inner revolts and confusions, devastating outbreaks of our fallen nature and our ego, and the like, so that sometimes the poor soul is overwhelmed by despair. But if the soul endures these sorrows, then its pride will become still more mortified, the soul will become still more truly and deeply poor in spirit (Matt. 5:3), learning to believe profoundly and truly that there is nothing and there can be nothing good in it on its own, without God. And at last (oh, the desired "at last") the soul will begin to pray from the bottom of its heart and with child-like sincerity: "Yours is the Kingdom; Yours is the power and the glory forever" (Matthew 6:13). amen! Our stubborn and obstinate will, yet long skilfully resisting and defending itself, will at last have to (oh, blessed "at last!") bow its head on the cross and immerse in Christ's death. Out of this death a quiet, pure life full of repose will be born. However I can say nothing about that life from experience.

At this point it would be necessary to set out how the soul must conduct itself amidst these sorrows; but it's not possible to give here one advice which can be applied in all cases. The soul responds to the different kinds of suffering, which also vary in their intensity, in a variety of ways. Here are a few general considerations.

1. While in a state of inner sadness, spiritual aridity and darkness, the soul should not strain itself trying to help itself violently, by changing inner and outer work, by deprivation of the body, by one's scrupulous examining of one's inner and outer situation and excessive reflections on that, a lot of read-

ing and the like. With all this, we will only harm ourselves and sink into even more darkness and disorder.

2. In particular, do not read books that, no matter how good they are, require a strong mental strain. One needs to read only what can nourish and strengthen one's heart, without stuffing one's head with many images; and read not much at a time, but moderately, in simplicity and silence.

3. Not give up when these sufferings last long, but humbly endure them until the Lord's hour comes. And when it seems to the soul that it can't do anything more for itself, let it still try to endure and bear the cross given to her.

4. To keep oneself, as diligently as possible focused within and, when there is no need, not deliberately appeal to one's feelings or, even more so, seek in the manifested world that joy and life of which God has deprived it at the moment.

5. Keep one's usual time for solitude and inner prayer, even though the soul would not want this, and it would even seem to it that the things get worse during its prayers.

6. Learn to distinguish correctly aspirations of one's inner man to God and opposing impulses of the fallen nature and the enemy (Heb. 5:14). By the manifestations of the latter, that is temptations, uprisings of sorrows, etc., softly and quietly "run away" from them with one's inner man to God, thus ignoring them and behaving as if they do not concern us at all.

7. Do not focus too much on yourself and your situation, but on God alone and keep yourself busy with Him, wholly entrusting and surrendering yourself, your soul and body to

Him, the faithful Creator and All-Beholder, in time and in eternity, and all this in Jesus Christ, by the power of His life-giving suffering.

It is difficult to mention in a short letter many other necessary details of such important truths of the inner life. You can see, beloved brother, that I just touched in general on something upon which a lot depends. As I mentioned at the beginning of the letter, I did not mean you personally , because, firstly, you understand all this better than me, and secondly, I don't know your condition accurately enough and God's guidance corresponding to it, which is in different circumstances as unique as people's faces. I hope God will give us another opportunity to speak with each other.

I entrust you with all my heart to the truly committed High Priest and Shepherd of our souls, Jesus Christ, May He accomplish His work in your soul. You too think of me, the feeble one, whose flaws only God knows.

LETTER 4. FUNDAMENTAL TRUTHS ABOUT HOW A PERSON IS SAVED AND SANCTIFIED BY GRACE

In the grace of the Lord Jesus Christ heartily beloved brother!

I've received long ago your kind letters of 23ᵈ November and 2ᵈ December and now, as far as my time and energy will allow me, I want to answer them.

As I could understand, your current state is described in the seventh chapter of the Epistle to the Romans. There is only one way out of this state, namely: an unconditional, whole-hearted immersion full of hope in the saving grace of God in Jesus Christ. Such an immersion brings death to the fallen pride, but it brings life and peace to the spirit (Rom. 6:3-1; 8:6)[1].

Sanctification and salvation by grace is accomplished not at all as easily as is generally thought[2]. When God's light and God's guidance truly embrace the soul, sanctification and salvation are seen quite differently. Then the Christian learns by experience that without inner purification, union with God is impossible (Matt. 5:8; Rev. 21:27). He desires and strives to fulfill everything required for salvation; but our deepest damage does not allow this to be achieved by his efforts alone. If a Christian stops here, then he gives up and falls into despondency. If he continues to live an ascetic life, then self-willed

---

1 This passage from Romans is about baptism. But since "baptism" in Greek means "immersion" ("β άπτισμα"), Tersteegen uses this second meaning (which is not alien to his native language: the German expression "sich taufen lassen" (to be baptized) comes from "tief machen", "plunge").

2 A reproach to Tersteegen's contemporary trends in Protestantism; see his treatise "Warning against spiritual superficiality and carelessness" in his book: Tersteegen, Gerhard. "The path of Truth"

righteousness manifests itself in him more and more, so that he begins to see that even his most elevated actions are stained with his hidden pride. And even if he reaches heaven for a while, then again he finds himself lying in the mud. What should he do? Trying to convince himself that a person in this life is doomed to remain a miserable sinner? It's a doubtful comfort. Trust in redemptive merits and the cross of death of Jesus Christ? Yes, it is absolutely necessary as these are the only foundation of our salvation. But Christ gave Himself for us, not only to redeem, but also to sanctify us (Eph. 5:26); and He did not come to loosen the law, but to fulfill it (Matthew 5:17). How to be? The Christian must go forward along the path of sanctification and holiness (1 Pet. 1:15-6; Rom. 6:22; 2 Cor. 7:13; Eph. 1:4; Col. 3:12; 1 Thess. 4:3), but he cannot. Hypocrisy or outward piety will not hold out for long... There is only one way left for a Christian - to accept this cross and with humble confession of his helplessness to renounce any of his self-willed action, so that God may perform His action in his soul. Here the Christian appeals fully to God, entrusts and commits himself to Him and then, believing in the grace and love of Jesus Christ granted to him, awaits that sacred hour when our almighty Saviour will reveal Himself to him and fulfill the required justification of the law (Rom.8:4). And that's exactly what the enlightened writers say, when they point to the inner prayer and focusing within and seeking strength, gaining it only from silence and hope in the Lord (Isaiah 30:15).

You may, dear friend, use on your own, without any embarrassment and fear, the advice of those enlightened prophets, but only with the following reservation. When writing about the elevated ways of purification, the souls, which follow those ways, mention that they didn't manage to appeal to God, to focus within, to deny themselves etc. in an active way. They actually had already achieved those milestones on the spiritual path, that they want to reach again by repeating their spiritual deeds. But since God made this knowledge [of their spiritual achievements] concealed for them they want to follow again those ways of purification.

Since the level of their spiritual achievements is far beyond your level, you will have to appeal to God in an *active* way.
This work, appealing to God, consists neither in the efforts of the mind, nor in the fervor and pressure of feelings, but in an inner crave and thirst for God in Christ, the aspiration of all the powers of the soul towards Him and peaceful reverent waiting for Him to reveal His presence to us. The basis here is a living faith that we have boldness to enter into the sanctuary by means of Jesus Christ's Blood, in a new and living way (Heb. 10:19) and that God in Jesus Christ has reconciled us to Himself (2 Cor. 5:18), as a result of which we can address Him in a child-like way, ask Him for anything and expect His action with confidence.
A Christian who is attentive to his inner life knows well that only by this work of child-like appealing to God, clinging to Him, entrusting himself to Him etc., his soul truly loosens itself from the fallen world, sin and all sorts of manifestations of his ego. His soul does not even look into the above mentioned, so that the sinfulness of those matters is not imputed to the soul, for the sake of Jesus, and thus the soul cleanses itself from all defilement of the flesh and of the spirit (2 Cor. 7:1) in the easiest and most reliable way.
Also, dear brother, you should not deliberately look for impurities and manifestations of fallenness in you; you will see them anyway, as far as it pleases God. Neither sin, nor our fall and damage must be the contents of our lives, but God, the Saviour and Friend of our souls, present with us in our hearts. When it occurs to you to be confronted with your own sinfulness, then endure it in God's presence like a sick child

who, tired of crying, lets his mother know about his suffering, just fixing his gaze full of pain on her. Scrutinizing ourselves makes us sick; gazing at God heals us. Embrace the awareness of your fallen nature as the true mercy of God and courageously endure it in the presence of the Saviour, not seeking consolation anywhere beyond Him. The Lord knows how and when to comfort us. Believing in this is an advancement (though not noticed by you) on the way to God; cowardice is the fruit of selfishness. Our infirmities and fallenness must affirm us in distrusting ourselves but never in disbelief in God, Whose pure love will burn all our infirmities faster than fire straw, when we put our trust in Him.

Behold, dear friend! I didn't tell you anything new. "The same passions afflict those who are your brothers in the world. (1 Pet. 5:9), although in varying severity and duration. Expect nothing from yourself, but everything from God's grace, which is so inwardly close to us. In such a position like yours, usual temptations arise when the soul thinks about itself as being the worst of all, that others do not know how bad it is in fact, and think too much good of it and the like. Ignore these thoughts and don't focus on yourself; we are all children of Adam. Your path has not yet been completed, but it goes in the right direction; and God's eternal love awaits only that you, and all of us, immerse in it as we are now.

Amen! May it be so!

Müllheim, 7th January 1744

II. On the receptive Acceptance of the Grace of God

LETTER 21. ON THE DIFFERENCE BETWEEN THE STATES OF BE-
ING UNDER THE LAW AND IN THE GRACE AND BETWEEN ACTIV-
ITY AND RECEPTIVENESS

Dear brother in Christ!

I am quite incapable of making long and detailed explanations. My inner state and the feebleness of my body do not
allow that, while it is impossible to answer your questions in
short. The writings of the illuminated souls which you possess in number, can satisfy you in this regard much more
than my letter.

You want to know what the exact difference is between the
states (as you write) of activity, or being under the law, and
receptiveness, or being in the grace of the Lord Jesus. Your
striving to find it out *exactly*, is actually erroneous. It is a
stumbling block in the spiritual life. Your, a bit exaggerated
thoroughness seeks to find support and conviction in the reason and relies on it too much. You want to establish yourself
on the accuracy and distinctness of spiritual concepts; but later on it can lead to delusions and obstacles when reality does
not coincide with the concept that you have already made
up. All our concepts remain extremely unreliable before we
try them out by our own practice. For this reason, and also
because God's guidance in relation to different people varies
extremely, I do not want and always avoid talking and writing
about the *precise* differences between the states of the soul.
Also if I had the proper knowledge of them and necessary
qualities that I lack. However, I will tell you what I know, for
you only, so do not share this with others, because due to
the weakness of my head I can hardly express my thoughts
properly. You seem to consider being under the law and ac-

tivity as the same state and being in the grace of the Lord Jesus Christ and receptiveness as the same state too. But in fact, judging by the text from Scripture, these are very different matters, although in some higher sense, at the end of the road, they probably can coincide. Being under the law is described in the seventh chapter of the Epistle to the Romans, while abiding in Christ, or in His grace, in the eighth chapter of this epistle. A Christian can reach this last state and be in the grace and yet be still very far away from the proper state of receptiveness in which it is not the soul which lives and acts, but Jesus Christ in it (Gal. 2:20). As the soul, which is in the grace, comes closer to God through *self-denial* and prayer, all its actions become more spiritual, simpler and gradually wane, while God's actions and the influence of the Spirit of Christ, on the contrary, grow more and more. I emphasize once again: there is no other means for the transition of the soul from the state of self-willed action to the state of receptiveness, that is when God lives in us, but, firstly, the denial of the will, desires and the reason of our fallen ego (Matthew 16:24), as well as all that is created (Matt. 19:29; Luke 14:33), and, secondly, prayer (Luke 18:1; 1 Thess. 5:17). He who establishes his heart and hope on something which is created or on himself, is neither under the law nor in the grace, but under fallen nature and is the child of this world. He who establishes his heart and hope only on God in Christ Jesus, is Christian, is in grace. Opening your heart to the fallen creation while thinking at the same time that you will put your hope in Christ too is a deceit and a false gospel. He who though he directs his heart and inner aspirations towards God and seeks the salvation of his soul, but has not yet put all his hope in Christ, and therefore undertakes various self-willed actions, in order to gain justification and peace with God, is under the law. Being under the law means that he lives in unceasing labor, flaws, fears and anxiety of his conscience, or just in self-blinding and self-righteousness.

All these states have their own grades and are often mixed up in the soul. The novice soul, which is under the law and craves repentantly and with true fidelity for Christ's grace, receives in one way or another, and even very soon, a taste of grace, sometimes considerable and comforting. But even then the soul is actually not under the grace of the New Testament and not in Christ (as it might think); it is only drawn to Him from the Father (John 6:44), strengthening in repentance, inner warfare and renunciation of the world. Sometimes the soul itself can, to a certain extent, generate such sensations or they can come from nature; then it is nothing but self-delusion. But by the proper order of things, after such a novice stays under the law, if the soul is sincere and faithful, it becomes truly absolved of its past sins through the Blood of Christ. More to it, a quiet and lasting confidence and sometimes an even more tangible proof of this arises in such a soul.

Then the soul is no longer under the law but under grace; it is in Christ, and it is attracted to Him, to the reception of His way of thinking and feeling (Phil. 2:5) and fellowship with Him.

But these are only the first steps of life in Christ; the soul is still not rooted and established in Him. The whole way of re-shaping oneself according to the life of Christ, according to His sufferings, death and resurrection is just beginning here. The Apostle Paul dwelt undoubtedly in Christ, yet even he says: "Brothers, I do not consider that I have already attained this. Instead, I do one thing: forgetting those things that are behind, and extending myself toward those things that are ahead, I pursue the destination, the prize of the heavenly calling of God in Christ Jesus." (Philippians 3:13-14).

The soul that has just begun to live in Christ puts its hope not yet wholly and exclusively in Him, but much more in itself, in receiving the grace and the use of grace's gifts, such as illumination, strength, virtues, which the soul gradually and imperceptibly ascribes to itself, as if these were its own properties. Then everything does not go the way the soul wants; spiritual darkness, emptiness and aridity seize the soul; it becomes anxious and despairs, and returns under the yoke of the law. Filled with thousands of fears, worries, anxieties it tries [in vain] to regain by means of self-willed actions its former pleasurable state. While the only way out for it is to resort to Christ alone, to surrender itself fully to Him and to entrust Him with the care for its deliverance, with all the soul's heart and hope, rejecting its own feelings.

Any other course of action only plunges the soul into painful self-willed care and fruitless self-willed activity. But if the soul turns to Christ, then God condescends in many ways to the soul and makes it feel grace again; but then again He will take away this feeling for a while, so that the soul would learn to truly abandon itself (Luke 14:26), to trust only in the Lord and let itself be ruled only by His Spirit. Thus, with many changes, most souls are purified and drawn to God.

Some other chosen souls, after they have already been sufficiently established in the Christian life, in due time are subjected to special purification, much more serious and severe. Namely, when they, already inwardly knowing God, and for this reason having no peace and joy outside of Him, are deprived not only of the feeling of grace and communion with God, but also of aspiration to anything divine. At the same time the deeply rooted human corruption, their ego and their complete inability to improve and preserve themselves, is revealed to such souls in an overwhelmingly powerful way. For some souls, this lasts a long time and seizes their whole being to its very foundations. Such a state of gross inner cleansing feels in many respects like a state under the law; but in fact it is completely different. Being under the law, the soul actively struggles with sin, seeking Christ in every possible way and hoping for His grace. But when undergoing the gross cleansing the soul willy-nilly must become receiving, that is give itself away (Mark 8:35) and completely entrust and surrender itself to God.

These elevated states of inner purification are very diverse, in accordance with the qualities of a particular soul and God's intentions concerning it.

In such states it is revealed for the soul in all clarity, how hard it is for a person to actually surrender himself to God's truth (which only deserves to be honored), truly deny any trust in himself and in something of his own, and completely and unreservedly surrender himself to [God's] grace, without expecting anything from himself, either here or in eternity.

If the soul, with God's help, will endure this purification, humbling (Matthew 18:4) and dying (John 12:24) and fully renouncing itself (Matthew 16:24), then it will be just as fully accepted by God; Christ becomes its righteousness and sanctification (1 Cor. 1:30) and the source of all its inward and outward actions. The soul is completely poor, feeble and small, but at the same time all-rich, invincible and bold as it is in union with the God Who lives in this soul, and it lives in Him (John 15:14; 1 Cor. 3:16; Gal. 2:20), as Christians more experienced than me can testify.

These elevated sorrows and sufferings replaced by the feeling of bliss when they ceased are especially characteristic of those chosen souls, which are attracted, or have the call of God, to go inward in order to achieve perfection in the inner life. Some get this attraction to turn inward earlier, some later; usually it emerges after the soul has passed its initial ardor and the accompanying excessive attachment to the sensible gifts of grace. The effect of this attraction can be seen first of all in the fact that the discourses of reason and self-willed-activity outside and inside become for the soul meaningless and unbearable. Instead there emerges in the soul a hidden aspiration towards inner and outer silence and detachment from everything. When the soul stays in a simple, reverent and loving aspiration in its attention towards God and His presence it feels good. As soon as the soul starts doing something else, like either reasoning about the spiritual matters or forcing itself to accomplish pious deeds or saying prayers aloud, it immediately plunges itself into disruption, restlessness and darkness. This is because all that is within the soul (Ps. 102:1) wants to give up everything and be only with God, etc. If the soul continues in such simplicity of silence and trust in God, then through this it becomes capable of receiving a greater, the most precious grace, that is when the soul loves God in detachment from everything and in inner peace and repose, and God from His side communicates to the soul His love and reveals Himself in it. Then everything that the soul seemed to have lost, comes back to it, and in great abundance and purity. But even after that, according to what God intends for us, He also still guides the soul through various paths of purification, humbling and dying of the former man (Eph. 4:22) for it to join in His purest Divine life in a more perfect unity with Him. I expose all this in a hurry and with a headache, so I can hardly formulate my thoughts. I therefore probably write, a lot of unintelligible, irrelevant, if not completely incorrect, stuff. Choose from it what is good for you, and ignore the rest.

I also want to say: when I say to you or to the souls kindred to you to leave self-willed activity and self-willed care, I do not in the least call for false freedom, idleness or free-and-easy carelessness. A Christian who gives his heart to God (Prov. 23:26) and completely entrusts himself to Him, loses fussy concern and fearful anxiety about himself, coming from self-love. However he can't give his heart to God and at the same time live in deliberate indulgence and entertainment.

He keeps himself aloof from all which is not God or of God; he loves prayer; he does, outwardly and inwardly, whatever is pleasing to God. He wants to be faithful to God and follow His ways neatly in everything: however without tormenting self-willed care, but having casted his cares on the Lord (Ps. 54(55):23). A Christian does not constantly examine himself, does not indulge in an incessant scrutinizing of his inner states, does not prescribe for himself all the time new spiritual exercises, does not want to acquire certain virtues of his own choice.

He bears or endures all his mental and emotional qualities and inclinations peacefully, also his inner sorrows, darkening and emotional numbness and insensitivity, weakness and temptations, still in a child-like manner resorting to God, lovingly reverent towards Him and praising Him in a quiet and meek spirit (1 Pet. 3:4). But of course, he does not allow himself to commit any sin.

If a Christian sins (or becomes aware of previously committed sins), then he does not fall into despondency, anxiety and despair, but immediately admits guilt, confesses his fall before God and endures grief and humiliation from sin peacefully.

And thus, out of this humility, a pure hope in God is born, when a Christian does not expect anything from himself, but everything from God only.

Here, dear brother, I have written a lot, but perhaps nothing which would satisfy you; anyway I'm not happy with this letter. I pray that the Lord Jesus Himself will rule your soul and guide you along true and better ways. You too pray for me; I really need this.

I remain your feeble brother.
Müllheim, 23ᵈ November 1740

May the Peace of God in Christ Jesus grow and become firmly established in our hearts!

Dear brother in the Lord!

I received your kind letter in a timely manner, but I could not respond immediately due to a sore head and some other circumstances. However, even without this, we are close to each other in spirit. The more we immerse in our good God, the purer and more effective becomes our communication until it is realized in the most perfect way in the age to come, where the prayer of the Lord Jesus will truly be fulfilled: "I am in them, and you are in me. So may they be perfected as one." (John 17:22-23). The Almighty gradually introduces us in this perfecting together through faith; we on our part must just humbly hope, receiving this great treasure solely due to His mercy.

I see, dear brother, that you too suffer from every distracting variety, from attention to earthly matters and "sticking to it"". They deprive you of your inner world, which, no matter how subtle and deeply hidden it is, is the gift of God and the greatest treasure, more precious than thousands of earthly kingdoms. Through this small world (for such it is in us for the most part) the Lord deigns to dwell, live and act in us, which is our only sanctification and salvation. The seed of this good tree has been sowed in all Christian hearts; but because it is small and deeply hidden, then - alas! - just a few notice it, give it all their attention and let it grow in them.

This seed is planted by the Lord Himself, and it ought to take root in us by its own power alone. A person who is coarse and focused on his animal nature (1 Cor.2:14) wants to see a lot, to strive a lot and to acquire a lot[3], otherwise, he believes nothing good will come out of it. This is because such a person cannot understand the pure and spiritual action of God (1 Cor. 2:14).

But he who chooses faith as his guide understands that the further, the more all this "examining, working on himself and to acquiring" must fuse into one, and eventually vanish. The plant we want to get fruit from, cannot constantly be dug up, stared at and groped as it doesn't need our inspection and actions. We just need to allow it to stay peacefully in the earth, and it will rise by its own inner strength. What is required of us is only not to impose a load on what is growing from this seed and protect it from weeds, harmful worms and insects. For the Lord to dwell in us and establish His peace in us, we must love inner and, as far as possible, outer silence, constantly stripping ourselves of the former man (Eph. 4:22; Col. 3:9) and being content and peaceful with respect to any position in which the Lord puts us at the given moment.

You feel, beloved brother, that the Lord (as you write) wants more and more from you in your current condition, that you would cling to Him with pure, unreasoning faith. Amen! But <u>let everything </u>be done as He Himself gives it, even if some-

3 "Acquire" implies in the spiritual sphere acquiring virtues through asceticism and scrupulous "watching, examining" oneself. Tersteegen does not deny the importance of this activity for the Christian neophytes, but warns against the conclusion that the entire Christian spiritual life would be reduced to this alone.

times its activity is very painful and not pleasant for our animal nature (1 Cor.2:14).

I remain brother, by the grace of the Lord, devoted to you in the love of Christ.

LETTER 23. STRIVING TO BE WHOLLY GOD'S SHOULD NOT BE REALIZED BY SELF-ACTION, BUT THROUGH THE LIFE OF CHRIST IN US. ABOUT OUR WORK FOR THE SAKE OF BEING GRANTED SUCH A LIFE

Dearly beloved brother in the Lord Jesus!

Your sincere desire is to continue to live in God's presence a new, pure life only dedicated to Him, is undoubtedly given to you by Him. Your conviction that such life can and must be lived in us only through Jesus Christ who lives in us (Gal. 2:20) completely coincides with mine. This is the work of Jesus, not of our ego. Exactly therefore for your desire of life in God not to remain just a desire, it should not come from impulses of emotions, but gradually move away from the animal nature (1 Cor. 2:14) and become focused onto the depths of the spirit, where it is generated. At the same time you must surrender yourself fully to God so that He Who planted in you this desire, would act in you according to His good will (Philippians 2:13).

Do not think that this is done in one moment, once and for always, and then you can allow yourself to lead a dissipated life and have fun again. By no means! If Jesus is to live in us, then *we* must stop living. We will have to constantly "prevent our fallen nature from living" , from sensuality and rationality, that is, to moderate their activity. And when we need to act, then act, obeying grace. By doing so, we will give a place in us to Jesus and His life, remembering at the same time that we cannot generate Jesus and His life in ourselves, it's none of our business.

Our business is only striving to give a place to Jesus in us, focusing within, with faith, hope and love. We should constantly adhere to this simple, calm focusing within and turning to

God, meekly and quietly surrendering ourselves to the guidance of Christ's love. Purely, simply and as God asks this (and not as "we"). In this very state work is necessary, without forming for ourselves in advance an image, but being in inner receptiveness waiting for the Lord to truly reveal us His life in us. Wait just like Christ's apostles were waiting, gathered in a house, for Pentecost (Acts 1:13; 2:1).
So, try to act less and less yourself and let Jesus act. Try to be like a child (Mt. 18:3), peaceful and embracing. There is a tendency in your soul to excessive severity and narrowness; don't give in to it. It would be nice if you had less distraction and more prayerful seclusion. However, do not undertake for now anything new; renewal must come to the heart, from the Lord. I am writing this in a big hurry.

Pray for me, as I pray for you!

Müllheim, 13th May 1739

LETTER 24. ABOUT ACTIVITY AND RECEPTIVITY. ABOUT PRAYER

Dear brother in Christ!

<...> No doubt that you have been given a vocation and the ability for inner life. However, the inner life is acquired not without death (Col. 3:5), into which man is introduced partly in an active, partly in a receiving, passive way. The active way implies abandoning and renouncing everything in which a person finds life, joy, and support outside of God (Luke 14:33). The receiving, passive way implies accepting everything (I emphasize: everything) that comes our way and that contradicts or mortifies [our former man (Eph.4:22)], in simplicity, as if it came from God, without contradiction, without worry and without wanting it to be different than the way it is. This includes inner insensitivity, aridity and obscuration, as well as involuntary distraction, perplexities of the mind, stirring of passions and such. All this (not consenting to the latter) needs to be endured calmly, and for the love of God. This is the way we enter into death; the Doers who lead us into it are on the outside the providence of God, filled with love; and from within, the Spirit of love, which is close to us in the depths of the heart and which draws and guides us to God according to our capacity, inner state and our situation in life. Let faith in this presence of God-Love (1 John 4:16), strengthening of this faith by frequent prayer, discerning and accepting the innermost drawing and calling (John 6:44; 10:3) which the Lord who loves us evokes in your heart, and following them completely entrusting yourself to Him, be your first and foremost pursuit. Through this inner silent fellowship with this Friend of our souls (Song 7:11) you will happily forget and leave yourself behind with all your infirmities.

But with such leaving yourself behind, it is necessary to understand properly your condition and capacity. Regarding you I want to say that you should not directly confront your enemies, that is your infirmities, temptations and such, or focus too much on them, but gently, albeit resolutely, distance yourself from them and forget them, but bow down to God and gaze at Him alone, holding on by faith only to Him.

Omitting your daily prayerful solitude, if it doesn't happen out of necessity, is harmful for you.

When praying, learn to make room for God and to surrender yourself to Him believing in His inner presence. Faith in the heartfelt closeness of God to us and the determination to be wholly His, constitute the core of prayer. While before God and with God you should be more receptive than active; but also in this everything should be left to the discretion of the Spirit of grace. You act too much by your feelings and reason. More precisely your sensual and rational nature wants to control excessively what is going on in your spirit. Your communication with God and prayers should be more intimate, gentle and inward. Since you lack this, you will not find peace, for the Spirit sees that your prayer is not quite genuine and sometimes too artificial. However, just remain steady and patient, even with aridity and darkness inside you.

First your pride must be mortified, then you will be able to feel the love of God without hinder.

Your feeble brother.

Müllheim, 17th May 1741
(Abbreviated)

LETTER 26. ABOUT THE FATHERLY KINDNESS OF GOD TOWARDS
THE SOUL, WHICH STRIVES FOR NOTHING ELSE BUT TO PLEASE
HIM. WHAT HAPPENS WHEN THE SOUL, IN A RECEPTIVE WAY, IS
PLEASED WITH HIM AND WITH ALL THAT HE DOES

In the grace of the Lord Jesus, beloved sister!

Since you and I will not see each other soon, I decided to
write you a few lines. Don't be embarrassed by the "ordinari-
ness" and "apathy" of your existence and do not think that
you are worse or more unfortunate than other souls, whose
inner life is bright and varied. One who strives to live according to God's commandments does not build his spiritual path
by himself. Christians commit themselves into the hands of
God, believing candidly that He Himself arranges everyone's
unique path, perfectly combining everyone's qualities and
properties with His intentions regarding each and everyone
of us. And in this faith not a single soul will be embarrassed
(Rom. 10:11), if only it desires nothing else but to follow the
Lord (1 Pet. 2:21) and wholly belong to Him (Acts 17:28). For
He, with truly paternal goodness and wisdom takes care of us
(1 Pet. 5:7), so that we do not have need to "get bogged down"
in ourselves.
And this, in fact, is the main thing that I want to tell you: strive
only to please the Lord or, in other words, that He may be
pleased with you.
And He pleases, and He is pleased with you when you are satisfied with Him and with everything He does for you, from
morning to evening, inwardly and outwardly, in the temporal
and in the eternal. Love and honor the ways of other souls
precisely because they are God's ways.
However love and desire for yourself your own way, also for
the reason that it was the good and wise Lord Who deter-

mined this way for you and Who guides you on it. For the utmost good for anyone is what the Lord gives him or her; and His giving is good for us when we are satisfied with it. You might be in a state of total "apathy", or more to it, of aridity, heaviness and darkness; but this is not sorrow at all, on the contrary, it is a great happiness, if only you are peaceful and contented with the fact that the Lord is pleased to allow all this to come on you. If you are at peace and pleased with God, then He is also pleased with you, and you are quite pleasing Him. When you fall into the abyss of your shortcomings, feebleness and fall, then peacefully accept such a defeat, because it is God's will. When you want to quietly and patiently bear this, but you can't do it, then also peacefully accept your revolt. When you find neither light nor virtue, no God, no grace inside you but just one continuous nothingness, then be satisfied with this nothingness, as far as it is possible for you, for through this you will be pleased with God and He will be pleased with you. On this path the soul truly dies with regard to the former man (Eph.4:22), almost without need to think about it; it has to renounce its fallen will, all its selfish props. It happens not in an active, but in a receptive way if only the soul consents to God and voluntarily accepts the work which He ceaselessly performs in it. O! Blessed is the soul that keeps for itself not a single image, not a single prop, but is content living only by pure faith in its Lord!

This state of all-satisfaction with the Lord must permeate also your outward life. I mean that we should accept peacefully everything the present day brings us (Matt. 6:34), even if we do not like it. For we have to do not with people, but with God, who governs the course of things so that it brings us the maximum benefit, even if we cannot comprehend it. Constant, gentle and humble surrender of our will to the will of God in everything that happens to us contributes in a miraculous way to our drawing nearer to God. On the contrary, inner discontent with the fact that the course of things is not exactly as we would like it to be, utterly darkens our spirit and leads it astray.

So, dear sister, unquestioningly surrender yourself into the faithful hands of the Lord, with regards to both the inner and outward man. We don't want anything else but to please Him; and this is exactly our salvation.

But if the merciful and wise Lord wants you to be poor and spiritually insensitive inside and speechless and meaningless outwardly or even to undergo sorrow, then say amen and consent to this too. Take comfort in the fact that thus you please God; and for the rest we don't care. May He bless, strengthen and sanctify your soul according to His good will!

I remain in Him your feeble brother (in haste).

Müllheim, 24th November 1741

III. On Prayer and Inner Work

May God abundantly pour out on us the spirit of grace and prayer, for the sake of Jesus!

In this grace, beloved friend and brother!

I often wanted to reply in detail to your kind letter! However I could do it only now and I think that it couldn't have happened before. Since I, though not answering your letter, nevertheless often prayerfully remembered you in love and unity of the spirit, then my delay thus turned into entrusting you to the Lord and praying to Him that He Himself would enlighten you through the anointing by His Holy Spirit and give you what I can say only a little and with great imperfection. Namely, I must speak to you about inner prayer, about which so many holy souls, guided by the divine light and their experience of communion with God, have written so abundantly and perfectly already. Truly, with fear and uncertainty and only because you inquire about this holy work of prayer, in order not only to know about it but to engage in this pursuit and to dedicate your precious time that you happily enough didn't waste on vanity, to God, to Whom you and all your time belong fully, I begin my letter. Oh, how I desire that also those around you would share your noble way of thinking and no longer lose themselves and the limited number of days of their lives in the flickering of the Fata Morgana of earthly life! May He who redeemed them with His blood and acquired these souls for himself as a property be merciful to them; and may He keep us faithful until death, so that no one steals our crown! (Rev. 2:10; 3:11).

So you ask, dear brother, what is inner prayer and how to practice it. I give my answer in two parts. In this letter I will, with God's help, try to briefly present to you the true foundation from the Gospel of this work of prayer. Thus I will point out to you the open door to the entrance of the innermost prayer room (Matt. 6:6), and at the same time describe in general the essence of this prayer. Concerning details, like e.g. how exactly the soul can do the prayer of the heart during the day or during hours of solitude, I will write to you, DV, in the second letter[4].

The inner prayer we are talking about here is the drawing of the soul closer to God in the name of Jesus and its abiding before His Face. In order to correctly understand and implement this, it is imperative that we, by grace and spiritual work, would imprint and constantly keep in ourselves as an unshakable foundation, a deep heartfelt feeling of the inwardly close presence of God. At the same time we must contemplate how He drew near to us in a special way in the name of His Son Jesus Christ, through His love for mankind, and that it is this drawing near of God to us that constitutes the foundation and the active cause of our drawing near to Him.

God is always present in us in a way that is incomprehensible to us. He fills heaven and earth (Jer. 23:24); "in Him we live, and move, and exist." (Acts 17:28); nothing is hidden from His eyes (Jer. 16:17). He sees our innermost thoughts, desires, inclinations and intentions (Is. 29:15); our entire heart is completely open and laid bare before Him (Heb. 4:13).

Most of all God, who is the Spirit (John 4:24), is close to our spirit, our inner man. Our spirit belongs not in this world, not in temporary things; it was created for God and for this reason it is able to have true fellowship with Him.

---

4 This intention of the author was not realized. See next letter.

Our spirit can and should be the temple and holy habitation of the Eternal Deity (1 Cor. 3:16); its very existence is to contemplate, to love and taste this blissful Essence and to rest in it.

For this it was created; for this it was given the necessary capabilities. So, God, as Spirit, is close to our spirit, and it is in fact there that He should be sought and acquired.

This Essence, which is worthy of all worship and love however, is not only present with us as God, but as *our* God in Jesus Christ; as "God is with us" (Matt. 1:23); like *our* - and my! - Saviour, Redeemer and true spiritual Friend (Song 7:11), Who cares for us (1 Pet. 5:7), loves us (1 John 4:19; Eph. 5:2), calls us to Him by His attraction (John 6:44), Who wants to live in us (John 14:23; 2 Cor.6:16) and be with us forever (Jer. 31:3), in spite of our unworthiness and wickedness, if we only open our heart to Him, and wholly entrust ourselves to Him. This is the great evangelical fundamental truth that a Christian must deeply imprint in himself and never forget, for it is the essence of our salvation.

I will dwell on this in some more detail. Man, fallen through Adam, is inwardly imprisoned by darkness and hell, which he carries in himself and with him in this life and which follow him after death too if he dies outside of Christ; God and His kingdom of love are very far away from him and firmly locked up for him. God in His holy eternity took pity on fallen man; it inspired His compassion to be revealed through the incarnation, suffering and death of his Son. And as our beloved Saviour, Jesus Christ, shed His blood for us and thus revealed the abundant love of God for mankind, so God, in the name of His Son Jesus Christ is unspeakably close to our hearts. The curtain has been torn apart through the death of Christ not only in the temple in Jerusalem. (Matthew 27:51). In our spirit too, as the Apostle Paul teaches us, the way was opened for us to the blessed, saving eternity (Eph. 2:18), so that God's mercy, grace, love, and communion with Him is available through the inner man even for the most ungodly sinners, if they would only turn to God.

Moreover, the Lover of Humankind, Who was born with us, precedes us; He stands at the door of the heart and knocks (Rev. 3:20) at it in every way; He is waiting for us and does not want anything else but that the sinner converts to Him and lives (Ezek.33:11). This is exactly the meaning of what is said: "Repent. For the kingdom of heaven has drawn near." (Matthew 4:17). And in the epistle to the Hebrews: "And so, brothers, have faith in the entrance into the Holy of Holies by the blood of Christ... So, let us draw near [to Him] with a true heart, (Heb. 10:19-22)."

And this drawing nearer, or coming closer to God through the name of Jesus is the very, the true inner prayer. I mean here not the first turning of a penitent sinner to God at his initial conversion, when he comes to God repenting and surrenders himself to Him in a certain general way, with a sincere decision to live from now on only for the one Who died for his sake and then resurrected. This first step of salvation is a precondition for life in Christ, and therefore I do not elaborate on it; I'm talking about a constant continuation of this drawing nearer to God of the soul which is already devoted to Him. For it is impossible for the hearts which were called by God and which entrusted themselves to Him, to be satisfied forever with the fact that they once, "generally" surrendered themselves to God when they first turned to Him.

Of course, Christians should now, and forever, consider their first conversion, if it was a true conversion, as a great blessing of God; but they cannot so to say settle down themselves on it and thus limit themselves. Over time, they feel in the depths of their inner man, an innermost urge to more and more fully and wholeheartedly strip themselves of everything which is not of God, to "consider everything to be a loss" (Phil. 3:8;

Col. 3:9) and to run and cling to God. They feel that something much more elevated, thorough and perfect is required of them, rather than their first conversion; their hearts tell them of the ways of God, that He wants to adopt them wholly and purely as His own (Rom. 8:15).

In some it is manifested strongly and clearly, in others faintly, covertly and vaguely; it largely depends on whether the soul is focused within and silent or distracted. Blessed is the Christian who is aware of God's holy calling in himself, and unconditionally, like a child, surrendering himself to it!

This aforementioned urge of the inner man emerges in us precisely because God, in the name of Jesus, is so benevolent and close to us. This God-Love close to us touches our spirit with His love, like a magnet touches iron, and draws it towards Him (Song 1:3). And from this our spirit feels such an aspiration and comes in such a motion, that it no longer can stop at nothing but God. If the soul preserves itself (1 John 5:18) by focusing within, if it will selflessly remove from its path everything that holds and stops the spirit, and will follow the urge of its inner man, having completely entrusted itself and everything that is its into the hands of God, then this urge will greatly augment the love that leads it to God. Just like streams of water flowing down, carrying everything which is in them in the ocean; or like a stone thrown from a height, rushing towards its foundation, towards the earth. And this is precisely what the pursuing of inner prayer means, namely: to be attentive to this attraction of the inner man, hold on to it in every possible way and follow it, while rejecting everything that is not God and of God, draw near to God in Christ and surrender yourself entirely to Him.

Then the spirit of a Christian becomes a temple, filled with the glory of God in its Holy of Holies; the temple, where the altar is the name of Jesus; the sacrifice is our heart, will and everything which can be called "ours"; the fire that never goes out is the love of God, which fans the aspiration of our love for God, and whose heat is truth and fidelity. In proportion to how much a Christian still has of this world, of its fall and of his ego, so much water is found in the firewood that is the sacrifice.

But firewood is gradually dried by that fire of the urge of the inner man I wrote about above. This fire shows itself in the deep groaning (Ps.37(38):10) of Christian neophytes and of those who follow the paths of repentance and inner suffering; over time, if the soul does not go astray this fire shows itself in the confidential "Abba, Father" (Rom. 8:15; Gal. 4:6) and similar cries of the heart that ascend to God as a pleasant fragrance; finally the deepest foundation of the soul is filled with indestructible peace, which guards our heart and mind in Christ Jesus (Phil.4:7). As long as there is a lot of moisture in the firewood and the sacrifice, it takes a strong fire, giving off a lot of smoke; then it burns cleaner and calmer and finally becomes an inwardly quiet and blissful fire of the Lord (Luke 12:49).

I express myself figuratively and, as it may seem, rather allegorically. But the matter is essentially exactly as I exposed it, and at the same time very simple and within touch. It is considered by people as something obscure and perplexing only because they are overly rational and remote from their inner man. Oh! My heart laments and cries for the blindness of people who take their deceitful and illusory deeds for something essential, and essential things for fantasies and delusion! But we were told in advance that the natural, fallen "man does not perceive these things that are of the Spirit of God." (1 Cor. 2:14). God have mercy on them!

I end the letter with the beautiful words of David, praising inner prayer: "Blessed is he whom you have chosen and taken up. He will dwell in your courts. We will be filled with the good things of your house," of your holy temple. (Ps. 64:5).

Amen! May the Lord lead us to come closer and closer to this blissfulness!

Desiring this in every possible way and cordially greeting you, your sincerely devoted friend and brother.

LETTER 31. WHAT IS INNER PRAYER, AND HOW DOES TRUE
PEACE AND TRANQUILLITY OF THE SOUL DIFFER FROM THE
FALSE ONE

Dear brother!

I couldn't whatsoever write to you earlier. You want to know
what real inner prayer is, and what is the difference between
true spiritual peace and tranquility and those false ones,
which come from our fallen nature. I prayed and continue
praying that God Himself would reveal this to you, protect-
ing you from the latter and leading you into the true peace
through the Spirit of Jesus Christ, the true Teacher of prayer
(Luke 11:1). If only you would surrender yourself to This
Teacher, as a true child of the heart, and trust in Him that He
would not let you go astray when you wholeheartedly want to
follow Him! As for me, I am becoming more and more unskil-
ful, and less and less able to speak and write on such matters
as I would wish; therefore, perhaps you will not be satisfied
with my answer.

Inner prayer is an appeal to God as to Him being present with
and alongside us in our heart through directing towards Him
our reverent attention and all our inner powers and staying
before Him, with Him and in Him, in accordance with the capacity and state of our soul.

Initially, our soul is more or less self-active in this (although
God always precedes it) and is volatile: at one time it feels
grace, at another time inner aridity and sorrow only, just as
all of us have experienced it. In the beginning the work of
the soul is predominantly initiated by feelings, and is therefore assertive, versatile, and needs diversity. It would always
abate after a while and needs to be re-started. Over time,
gradually (if the soul does not abandon its path), its work of

prayer becomes more quiet, more inward, less diverse and multi-subject; the soul needs less and less to constantly urge itself to prayer, and, finally, as it were "loses" itself in prayer, since God Himself acts in us still more, so that it is no longer "I, but truly Christ, who lives in me." (Gal. 2:20).

The teacher and instructor of this inner prayer is the Spirit of Jesus Christ; the one praying must entrust him/herself like a child to His guidance and follow Him unconditionally. He touches our soul and our love and makes us aware of the " drawing of the Father" (John 6:44) which is some hidden and subtle attraction towards the depths of our heart, towards the Source of our life (Ps. 35(36):10; Luke 17:21). If we do not follow this "attraction", then we will never come to God. We cannot generate this "attraction" from ourselves, it is [granted] grace. However we might stifle, hinder and resist the grace already granted to us it if we too much, and unnecessarily, abandon our prayerful staying in our inner self. Even more so, by directing our love and heart's aspirations to other matters and be carried away by them.
There is no need to speak of even more subtle obstacles at this time.

Already from the above mentioned it should be clear to you what is false peace of mind and tranquility. The first case is when one who during his/her prayer deliberately and consciously allows his thoughts and desires to abandon God and turn to something else. The second case is when the praying one manages in some way to keep his thoughts at a certain distance from external matters and forgets them. But he allows his heart and will to be in captivity of the created world, and as such doesn't really surrender himself to God and does not really appeal to Him. Although such a person (due to, say, some by nature underdeveloped intellect or vacancy of mind) is not always aware of the fact he is fixed on other matters; but anyway, he does not have God and the divine [matters] as object of his attention. More to it, he doesn't really want this. The third case of false rest and peace is when a person completely abandons prayer, and under the imaginary pretext that he has already completely entrusted and surrendered himself to God, lives in comfort day after day, letting his heart, thoughts and feelings roam around the world just as they please. Such false spirituality and imaginary freedom is easily avoided if the soul will properly give place in itself to hearing the voice of grace and the Spirit (Heb. 3:14-15).

When our good God deigns to reckon us among His friends (John 15:14), then He takes away from us any desire for diversity in inner life and in the remembrance of God, especially during prayer. The Christian can no longer say something to the Lord or ask something from Him in so many different ways and regarding so many subjects as before, when he did it according to his own understanding only. Everything fuses in his prayer into a single, reverent attention full of love towards God, Who is also present in his inner and close to him, and Whom he worships in silence. He has no words but perhaps just a word of love, to say it to God.

Abiding in such a not false, genuine silence, the Christian acquires a kind of innermost well-being, without examining its causes; he feeds on it, not knowing where this food comes from (John 3:8), etc. If something like this happens to you, dear brother, then do not let yourself be confused that this is a delusion, which [confusion], unfortunately, happens to many souls. On the contrary, this is precisely the way which leads the Christian into genuine prayer when God is dwelling in us (John 14:23) and even into becoming one spirit with Him (1 Cor. 6:17); and on this path the soul gains unspeakable blessings.

However another inner state, when we do not feel any joy during inner prayer and appealing to God, but only aridity and emptiness; or when the rational and sensual part of the soul suppresses and clouds us with a thousand distracting fantasies, confusion, etc, is not wrong or false either. When this happens to us, we must not pay attention to it, but calmly, with patience (Luke 21:19), entrust it to God. Then our spirit will not be affected by these storms, and it will remain in its place and in his work as calmly as it is possible for it. It is like a child when awakened in the arms of its mother by some inner disturbance or noise from outside, turns back to the mother's breast, so that, having received nourishment from it, immerses again in a peaceful state. I want to say that a Christian comes out of such temptations with true peace and tranquility when he renews in himself faith in the inner nearness of the Lord, loving reverence for Him and complete surrender to Him. When he testifies his love before Him either with a prayerful word expressing that he desires nothing else but God only (Ps. 72(73):25); or worship, glorification and pleasing to this perfect Good [God] through certain works of love; or when he adheres to that which benefits his soul, and so on. All this a Christian does unsophistically, quietly, simply: truly will his soul resume its former peace and nourishment through such work. If after a while it turns out that God does not want to set the soul at rest, then the Christian understands from this and believes that it is appropriate for him to endure all this inner aridity, obscuration and despondency. Such endurance, which comes from unconditional union with the will of God, is in itself the most beautiful prayer. But at the same time, one must be very alert, so that , through one's arbitrary absent-mindedness or deliberate unfaithfulness to God, one does not give on one's part a real reason for falling into inner darkness and emptiness. If this still happens, then a Christian must humble himself and confess his sin before

God, after which he calmly continues to go his own way, as if there was no stumbling block at all.

Perhaps I will confine myself to what has already been said, without touching on other types of prayer or the various subtleties of God's guiding and teaching, which in inexperienced people may arouse suspicion of delusion, idleness, excessive freedom, etc. The main thing is what I said at the beginning: the self-initialization and independent action of the soul in conjunction with the soul's faithful following of the Christian path weakens more and more. It becomes replaced, as it were, overcome by the action of God, so that the all-consuming life of Jesus is revealed in us (2Cor. 4:10). The actions of God gradually become clear to the soul, and cast aside the soul's doubts whether it should accept them and not hinder them by an action of its own. It can also be said that God powerfully takes the soul into His hands, so that it willingly hands over to Him the guidance of all her actions. As for the purification and inner sorrows: the soul humbly accepts all these, it endures, it suffers, it loves, and acts as described above.

In short, do you want to engage in inner prayer and avoid any kind of false spirituality? May your prayer always be accompanied by constant renunciation of all the created and of yourself (Matt. 16:24) according to the instructions of the Spirit and Providence of God, so that you could purely love God and entrust yourself to Him alone. Also avoid all the vanity of this world and excessive diversion in feelings, thoughts, deeds, conversations and dealings with people, so that you are not blinded and distracted from God, but walk before Him and in His presence, becoming pleasing to Him, as a true child of Abraham (John 8:39). To this I wish both you and myself the fullness of Jesus' grace and true guidance of His Holy Spirit.

Behold, beloved brother in Christ, I have written much more than I was intending to. No doubt you will be surprised at

my boldness, that I, though foolish and full of shortcomings, speak of such things, about which great and enlightened souls have written with much light and grace. Well now! Accept only that what is in accordance with their writings; however, I did feel an inner impulse to tell you all this.
Pray for me! And I will do my best to pray for you.

May the Lord Jesus live in your soul; in Him, greeting and embracing you, I remain your devoted brother.

Müllheim, 1st July 1740

LETTER 32. ADMONITION CONCERNING THE TRUE STILLNESS OF
SPIRIT, OR HEARTFELT PRAYER

Dearly beloved brother in the Lord!

May the sweetest Child Jesus lead us these days into the man-
ger of our hearts to teach us the true Sabbath (Ex. 20:8), which
consists in nothing else than that He would reveal and manifest Himself in us. Then His presence generates in us reverent
abiding before Him, which causes all the forces of the soul to
fall silent. Until this happens, we, for our part, prepare ourselves for this by prayer and a comprehensive rejection of the
life of our ego. A Christian cannot hope for an essential, pure
and permanent silence of the spirit if he/she, taught from
within by the guidance of the Spirit (1 John 2:27), and from
outside by actions of God's providence regarding him, will
not put the life of his ego to death (Rom. 6:2; Col. 2:20; 3:3, 5).
The one who died is silent; while earthly life cannot be silent.
Thus, this heartfelt Sabbath obliges us by heartfelt prayer,
to try to place ourselves by means of our faith in the inner
presence of God, abandoning (through detachment, without
applying violence to ourselves) all extraneous thoughts and
impressions. At the same time we gently, but resolutely direct
our will together with the scattered and squandered aspirations of our love towards the Lord present in us , entrusting
all of ourselves and all that is ours to Him. Doing the above we
should stay before Him and with Him in this focusing within
as peacefully and for as long as we can.
This quiet, peaceful and reverent silence in God's presence
requires more of us than is usually thought, because we seldom feel the fruit from this at once. Often a Christian, as it
seems to him/her only loses his/her contentment and peace,
not to mention the fact that this practice itself seems some

kind of idleness. But in this practice we accomplish that very "one thing" which is necessary (Luke 10:42) and thus we accomplish everything. This practice transforms us in such a way that the Lord can quieten and pacify us in essence by His attraction and Divine actions.

We must be absolutely faithful to God's "drawing" (John 6:44), which, with due attention, we feel during our everyday activities and while being amongst other people too.

This faithfulness doesn't prompt us to pursue e.g. a big number of spiritual deeds but to gaze reverently as often as possible at God while focusing within. This is exactly what the Lord, Who draws us nearer to Him, wants from us and teaches us.

As for the disturbances and agitations of thoughts and feelings opposing this work: just do not pay attention or focus on them, but calmly endure them. And if you happen to become distracted involuntarily, then you need to immediately take up the above practice of faith and place yourself in God's presence: either by peacefully gazing at the Lord Who loves us, or reverently worshiping Him, or entrusting yourself to Him, etc.; but everything should be done quietly and simply. Let your reason, feelings and thoughts do what they want; and even if they would plague you greatly and for a long time, endure without being overwhelmed and without answering them. Just abide quite peacefully in your prayer and rejoice, that you were honored to suffer insult on behalf of the name of the Lord Jesus (Acts 5:41).

It is in this kind of spirit that "man will go forth to his work and to his activities, until the evening." (Ps. 103:23), striving even in the midst of his pursuits to be in the presence of the Friend of our souls (Song.7:11) and having not seven other tasks in his head, while fulfilling his current task.

Here, dear fellow, I wanted to write just a few lines, but look how much I've spread myself!

I welcome you and remain your devoted brother.

Müllheim, 20th December 1742

Beloved sister in the Lord!

I received both your letters in good order. I'm glad with your decision you wrote about, that is to be wholly of God and to belong entirely to Him. Now get back to your Christianity, so that at last something solid and complete might come out of it. Firmly believe that God will certainly give you strength for this when you turn to Him in such a state of mind. This particular state of mind, to always abide in secret with God and humbly grant Him to rule over you, should be as the foundation of your solitary prayer, so accompany all your studies and your dealing with people.

You complain that you spend your time of prayer to no avail. Then start doing this so: when retreating to your solitude, heartily entrust yourself to God and ask Him, that He may bless the coming hour and be with you. Then take the book that most awes you and read it, as in the presence of God, carefully and quietly, so as not to miss a single word. Relate all you read to yourself, take in the contents most fully and store it in your heart. If while reading something catches your attention, especially moves you and carries you to God and to His presence, then read no further, but give place to this touch of grace and begin to pray, that is, to abide in your soul with God, worship Him, entrust yourself to Him, renounce your ego, etc. When what has caught your attention ceases to nourish you and the inner reverent immersing within is no more there, then start reading again in your initial mood. Spend in this manner half of the time appointed by you for solitude; dedicate the other half to prayer alone, without reading; as reverently and thoroughly as you can, disregarding in what state you are, may it be inner darkness or light, aridity or enjoying God's grace.

At the end of the prayer, before you return to your usual activities, thank God heartily for this hour; restore your resolve to be faithful to the Lord, at the same time denying your fall and selfish life; ask God to always be with you and not to leave you amidst your everyday pursuits.

Then abide reverently with God and do all your works for the sake of His love and for His glory, in that very spirit, which I've described at the beginning of the letter; and preserve yourself (1 John 5:18), so as not to give to the fallen nature and ego any nourishment.

My sick head does not allow me to write further. I recommended sister N. the same rule of reading and prayer.

Be careful so as not to engage in these spiritual activities routinely or out of habit, as well as in all your mundane affairs.

On the one hand do not succumb to the laziness of nature, on the other hand, do not allow excessive self-strain. Oppose these extremes with the child-like fear of God and constantly placing yourself in the presence of God.

Remaining your devoted brother.

Müllheim, 18th February 1737

Beloved sister in the Lord!

Your last letter has been received safely. We[5] always read,
with heartfelt sympathy, about your inner state; so when you
write to us, do it simply and frankly. Then we will also be able
to respond to your benefit.

Concerning your present situation, here are a few words of
exhortation. You complain that you don't surrender, in sufficient measure, to grace, and you listen, too much, to the voic-
es of strangers (John 10:5); that you lack the lasting peace of
Christ; you are often anguished inwardly; also that your selfishness poses obstacles, in many ways; and that everything is
just too messy and chaotic.

In order to organize everything properly, it is mandatory
that you not miss your times of solitude for prayer and for
focusing within—unless there's some good reason. Be aware:
When cloudy water is constantly shaken, it cannot become
clean and transparent. Often, we think that we are completely
focused within, and therefore it not so necessary to retreat
into solitude. But we don't know ourselves well enough; and
the distractions of which we are not conscious are all the
more dangerous.

So, retire regularly at a certain time of the day, rejoicing in
this as in some fine meal; enter your room (Matt. 6:6) and
offer to your Friend and Beloved (Song 7:11; 2:16) all your

5 Here and below: if the letter is written on behalf of "we", then Gerhard Tersteegen and Wilhelm Hoffmann are meant (see Preface about
him). During the first years of his counsel in correspondence, Tersteegen often used the advice of his spiritual mentor and friend; some
letters are written on behalf of both of them.

heart and your entire will. Watch with all diligence, solely to offer yourself to Him wholly; and then gaze upon God, as being present with and alongside of you, and trust that He will certainly look upon you. God will reveal your infirmities to you and work by means of His grace, as the potter works on the clay that he shapes in his hands. If you become distracted in the process, despite yourself—that is, by succumbing to one or another manifestation of selfishness or fallenness, or the like, then do not be cowardly; but with all sincerity, prostrate yourself before the Lord, so that He will abolish all of this. Remove your inner self from all impurity—however, without undue passion or strain. Remove yourself, forget about it, and be restored to full love, with hope gazing at God, Who is with and alongside of you—your only treasure, refuge, and comfort.

When you get back to your everyday work, continue to abide in the company of this Friend. Look often at Him in faith, as unfailingly co-present with you; do everything before Him and for Him, out of love for Him and in glorification of Him, no matter how small your work may be; and rejoice if you meet with an opportunity to accomplish a difficult task or suffer for Him.

Let this sweetest work, that is, child-like abiding in the co-presence of God, be your main pursuit, in accordance with which your other pursuits must be prioritized. If you deviate from this plan, then return to it, as soon as you became aware of the deviation. Then you will know by experience, with how much fidelity and love the Lord leads you, as He shelters you "in the way that a hen gathers her young under her wings" (Matt. 23:37), how He strengthens, heals, and cheers you up, which is impossible to express in words.

May He let you understand this, and you shall want for nothing, forever!

LETTER 35. ABOUT THE SIMPLE AND EASY ART OF TRUE PRAYER

Beloved sister in the grace of God!

You do well to pray as much and as diligently as you can. Continue this unceasingly, and God's precious promise will certainly come true for you: "Ask (that is, pray), and it shall be given to you." (Matt. 7:7). There is no art, on earth, simpler and easier than true prayer; it is actually not an art at all, and if we think that we cannot pray properly, this is a sign that we do not yet understand what prayer means. To pray means gazing at God, Who is present with and alongside us, and opening ourselves to Him, so that He may gaze at us.
What could be easier and simpler than to open your eyes and see the light that surrounds us on all sides? God is incomparably more present to and with us than visible light: "in Him we live, and move, and exist (Acts 17:28)." He penetrates us; He is closer to us than we are to ourselves. To believe, with simplicity, in this and, as far as it is possible, to remember this, is the very prayer itself. And how hard can it be to let yourself be inspected by such a good Physician, Who knows our state incomparably better than we ourselves? When we get to prayer, we do not need to communicate to God, neither about this nor that, nor to spin around before Him, showing all our facets, nor to meditate and feel deeply, all the time, precisely what we would like to say to Him.
We have only to proclaim to Him, simply and briefly, what we are and what we want to be. It's not even necessary to say this to Him, but only to place ourselves before the eyes of the loving Lord, who is present with and alongside us; we place ourselves not casually, but rather in such a way as to abide

with Him and before Him for a sufficient period of time, so
that He may, so to speak, deeply examine and heal us.

Be careful not to pretend to be, before His face, other than
you really are. If you find yourself distracted, darkened, or
shackled by spiritual insensibility, or such things, then tell
this to God in simplicity; let Him see your weakness, and this
will be true prayer.

If during prayer some lethargy or natural drowsiness comes
upon you, cheer yourself up a little and humbly turn again to
God. If, during kneeling, sleep overcomes you, then it's better
to stand on your feet. Also, in such cases, you can read something for a change.

In short, help yourself in any way you can, but do not allow
yourself be carried away by auxiliary means—and do not forget your main goal, prayer, and constantly return to it, again
and again. The more you reject self-will and selfish desires,
the easier prayer will be for you.

May the Lord establish the prayer by His grace in your soul
and in mine! I remain your feeble, like-minded friend in Him.

Müllheim, 4th December 1731

LETTER 36. TO THE SAME PERSON. TRUE LOVE FOR GOD IS NOT
HARMED BY ANY CHANGE. IT IS NECESSARY TO GAZE AT GOD
AND APPEAR BEFORE HIS EYES

Let Adam die, and let Jesus lives in us!

Beloved sister in the Lord!

I've received both of your kind letters. I am very pleased. It is
worthy that you are firm in willingly renouncing everything
(Luke 14:33). "Love the Lord your God from your whole
heart, and from your whole soul, and from your whole mind,
and from your whole strength" (Mark 12:30).
May the Lord Himself preserve and fulfill this in you!
No alteration of light and darkness, or spiritual aridity and
blessed states, or such things, can harm us in the least, as
long as the aforementioned state of our soul remains unshakable. If we, however, (may the Lord spare us from this!) lose
this state, then we should humbly and patiently make the intention, again, to renounce everything and to love God. We
should repeat this effort of ours until the lost is regained, by
the grace of God; and then hold on to it and not allow anything within ourselves to oppose it.
In response to the rest, I will repeat what was said in my previous letter. Gaze at God and open yourself to be examined
by Him, both during your prayer retreat and outside of it.
This means: At every time and in every place, put yourself by
means of faith in co-presence with God, "which surpasses all
knowledge" (Eph. 3:19), filled with love. Bow, contemplate,
love, and honor Him, revere Him, and abide with Him and
His infinite perfections, as long and to such an extent as you
alone can.

Expose everything, before His eyes, all that is in you; do all your work as if before His face, for His glory, out of love for Him—without any other consideration. Gently avert your gaze from everything that arises in you, good or evil, and by faith turn all of this over to God, Who is co-present with and alongside you—for His consideration and judgment.

In short, gaze at God and at all that is His, and He will gaze at you and all that is yours. Whoever looks at himself, a great deal, and at what is his, is liable to fall into cowardice and despondency, or, again, to be puffed up by arrogance.

May the Lord deliver us from this. I remain your loving brother in Christ.

Müllheim, 9th February 1732

LETTER 39. ON THE NEED FOR PATIENCE IN PRAYER AND FO-
CUSING WITHIN, ESPECIALLY IN TIMES OF INNER ARIDITY, DEV-
ASTATION AND DARKNESS

In the grace of the Lord Jesus, precious and beloved brother!

Although we correspond, just a little, with you, I can say in
simplicity, before God, that I have a great affection for you and
rather appreciate our "unity of the Spirit within the bonds of
peace" (Eph. 4:3).
Your last letter of January 17 rather appealed to me. You over-
estimate me in it; but I take this as a sign of your love and as
an encouragement to work on improving myself in the Lord.
I always commit you, in my prayers—and the state that you
revealed to me—with brotherly regard, to the Lord and His
grace, which I desire for myself, too.
Patient constancy in the practice of prayer, and focusing within, are very important for a Christian; this can be convincing-
ly confirmed, along with other things, by the intensity of deceit and the tricks with which our enemy, and tempter, tries
to distract us. And when he does not quite succeed in doing
so, then he sends lethargy and laziness upon us during our
prayer time. The enemy knows very well that his kingdom of
darkness, in our souls, is being destroyed, exactly by this holy
work, through which the light, love, and life of Jesus are gradually and imperceptibly poured into us. He knows, too, that
the flowers and fruits of our most beautiful virtues wither,
if he manages to cut them off from this root, which is prayer
and focusing within.
Lord Jesus Christ is the only Mediator (1 Tim. 2:5), Who
brings the divine life and powers, again, to us and into our
human nature, which has fallen from its rank and become as
if dead to all good.

While being in heartfelt prayer (in which faith, love, hope, and so on, are combined and focused), we unite with Him and we are strengthened in Him. In this prayer, our yearning and thirst for God and our inner striving towards Him become, as it were, the roots, which receive from Jesus both juice and strength, although we cannot always clearly see and feel how this is done. Therefore, we will strive to pray without ceasing (1 Thessalonians 5:17) and to focus within in the heart. A prayer, though imperfect, with many flaws, is still more salutary than even the most-comely diversion. The enemy catches our attention, and with many shiny, imaginary benefits directly pulls and pushes us towards them—with the only purpose to make us to abandon the prayer.

Your letter, dear brother, has further confirmed what both my experience and the experience of many Christians have taught me, namely, that the adversary makes special use of times of spiritual trials, inner emptiness, aridity, and darkness in order to divert the soul from the correct performance of prayer, and, as a result of this, to divert us from the Source of our strength. This occurs precisely when the Lord leads us into the stage of spiritual maturation, when we begin to understand how we must come out of our former man (Eph.4:22) and, holding onto the Lord alone, cling to Him.

You write, that you can no longer carry out your prayers as before, in a customary way.

The proper way to carry out prayer, in such situations, is to stop attempting to hold on, stubbornly and with self-will, to what the Lord wants to alter or to take away. We are to make it so that we calmly and humbly acknowledge what has been revealed to us by the Lord, about our fallenness and poverty. Then we are to sacrifice our own opinions, designs, and desires in favor of God's plans and commandments, so that His good becomes our prayer, our opinion, our design, and desire. Then, from such a sense of abandonment and loss, we will in time receive a great acquisition. We will become capable of a deeper and purer focusing within, a true prayer and union with God, which is exactly the intention of God regarding us. Our poverty and fallenness mean mainly that we, being permeated and impregnated with selfishness, seek ourselves and what is ours (Philippians 2:21), most of all, when we are convinced that we seek God. When we find neither light nor joy on this path, we come to the conclusion that we cannot reach God. Then we fall into faint-heartedness, and despondency, and begin to look for nourishment and support for our ego, somewhere else, because we cannot find that in God and His benefits. O Lord! How undignified is such a state, for hearts that have dedicated themselves to pure service toward You and Your love!

Destroy this very foundation of selfishness, so that we, serving You, truly seek not ourselves, but You; not our own delight, but that which is pleasing to You, for You are our all, and in You, and not in us, lies all our salvation and bliss!

Before the day of Pentecost, the disciples of Christ couldn't stay in peace and quiet and silence for long without the physical, the visible, presence of Jesus. 'I am going fishing' (John 21:3), says Peter; the time of loneliness dragged on him painfully. It happens with us as well. We try 'to catch fish' in some book, some person, or so on, and it's by the grace of God if we don't catch anything that night, but instead the Saviour will meet (John 21:3-4) and shame us, as beloved disciples, showing the futility of our self-willed quest.

Having experienced such fear and shame, I testify, with immeasurable gratitude to God's long-suffering and goodness, what I have learned through it: the omission of inner prayer causes a great harm to the Christian. Especially in times of darkness, inside, and spiritual aridity, it is very easy to lapse into this temptation. This harm is not recognized directly; but gradually man deviates from God's way, and sometimes so far that he is almost not able to find the strength to return to it.

A soul without prayer is like a lost sheep without the shepherd. Our enemy knows it; he takes advantage of the murky and devastated state of the soul, in order to alienate it from the Shepherd. He cunningly weaves its webs, throws the soul into confusion and doubts, presents to the soul all sorts of choices, and encourages it to launch a variety of changes, for instance: Why not to undertake this or that spiritual practice? Why not change the external situation? Why not visit one or another place? Why not move to another church community? And so on, and so forth. Many sincere souls, both in modern times and in former times, have been deceived by this. They have lost their way in this dark night.

This should serve as a warning to us that, when we are in a state of spiritual obscurity and devastation, we wouldn't change anything in our life, but instead stay where we are and how we are.

And then let us take heart in the name of Jesus, let us begin again, from the point where we stopped; and let us be zealous in the Lord, as it was before our going astray! God's mercy uses everything, even our mistakes and sins, for our benefit (Rom. 8:28); may His wisdom be praised and worshiped! Later on, seeing the back of Him (Ex. 33:23), we will understand the best way to use those mistakes to our advantage: to lay them down as the foundation of our true humility (although, of course we should not justify our sins under this pretext, but avoid them with all diligence Rom.6:12). Our "nothingness", about which we hear, read, and think gives rise to a certain humility, but it is such a kind of humility that sometimes makes us very arrogant.

However, our "nothingness", as learned by our experience, does not leave even the slightest shelter for selfishness: a person knows for sure that he is unhappy, and miserable, and poor, and blind and naked (Rev. 3:17), and begins to truly recognize his fallenness. Many people say that self-righteousness is completely alien to them, but that is because they have little or no righteousness at all. With respect to the truly pious souls: the poison of self-righteousness inevitably creeps into them at the beginning of their Christian path. As the result of this poisoning, their zeal, self-denial, virtues, and use of God's gifts are, imperceptibly, established on the basis of their self-righteousness and self-confidence, instead of being based only and exclusively on God. But over time, our loving Saviour opens our eyes, by means of our own dirt (John 9:6, 11), so that we may give all honor to His miracle-working right hand, while keeping for ourselves the coming debacle of our self-confidence.

The experience of our infirmities, fallenness, and our all-embracing nothingness, however, should not give rise in us to faint-heartedness, but rather give us a reason to free ourselves from ourselves, to leave ourselves behind, and, as we become more and more pure, therefore we, all the more, essentially (Matt. 5:8) cling to God, so that He may fill us with Himself, and thus became in us everything that we, by no means, can by ourselves either have or achieve. God wills to unite with us in such a way that "nothing that is of the flesh should glory in His sight" (1 Cor.1:29), but that He alone "be our wisdom and justice and sanctification and redemption" (1 Cor. 1:30).

So, dear fellow, you see that by leaving oneself behind, and stripping off oneself—while "seeing the back" of Him (Ex. 33:23)—we receive a genuine knowledge of our fallenness. This leads and makes us capable of the most elevated prayer and unity with God.

Be blessed by the marvelous and infinite "kindness and humanity of God our Savior" (Titus 3:4) in Christ Jesus, our Lord!

Since, while writing, I was constantly distracted, and visitors with all kinds of business often interrupted me, this letter came out somewhat uneven and unclear. I just want to assure you of my love—by approving what God's anointing teaches you (1 John 2:27). Let's not miss, my fellow, the unceasing learning in the school of our only Teacher of truth, Who is sinless; in order for us to become like small children, more and more, in the heart! Oh, what this anointing teaches us is the absolute truth, and there is no other truth but this one!
I greet and embrace you in the spirit of love. Pray for me, as you remember me; and I, by grace, will do diligently the same. Greet our brothers and sisters in Christ in N for me. I often send prayers with well-wishes to all of you: May the Lord Jesus warm and enliven our hearts with His sweetest love! Amen!
Still I am very weak and cannot write much; for this reason. I now end this letter too.

I remain in grace your feeble fellow who is sincerely devoted to you.

Müllheim, 12th March 1750

IV. About God's Peace

Letter 40. A sign of being surrendered to God is spiritual peace and tranquillity

Beloved brother in the Lord!

How can we determine whether we've surrendered ourselves fully, within our capability, to God?
It can be checked easily and simply. When we entrust ourselves completely and truly to God, then peace that is the resting of our spirit in God falls upon us; one is inseparable from the other. In the normal course of life (that is, outside the period of temptations and trials) all the forces of the soul devoted to God are in peace and quiet, as if motionless. When the will is to act, it operates freely, calmly and peacefully. The spirit is turned to God and is open to Him and remains so without compulsion and efforts for the necessary length of time. The duration of this inner, essential and pure state depends on the degree of the extent of self-surrendering to God. A soul, especially at the beginning of the path, easily loses this state, so that it hardly lasts longer than the time that the soul is prayerfully deepened in the heart.
A description of this in so few words may not be very clear, therefore it is even easier and more reliable for everyone, whatever his or her capability is, to do like this: the soul, to the maximum possible to it extent, peacefully places itself in the heart before the eyes of God and then, but without making up any image! directs its quiet and reverent inner gaze at God, Who is so close to us, letting Him determine what else outside and inside of us is not yet offered to Him, and at the same time, wishing sincerely and cordially to entrust to Him all that is of us, inside and outside of us.
The soul abides in the light of truth while being in this simple awaiting, without upsetting itself by examining and search-

ing for interpretations, as long as God's grace allows it to be, moving away at the same time, gently and calmly from any distracting thought, feeling or desire. Then the soul is still introduced deeper into the pure order of God, the mind of Christ (1 Cor. 2:16) and thus completely entrusts itself to Him. The outward rigor is good in so far as it facilitates inner life. What is needed here is sincere, not hypocritical renunciation in spirit from everything that is not God and of God. A modest home environment and in all our manifestations helps a lot; more, than one usually thinks.

Your attraction to silence and withdrawing from the hustle and bustle comes doubtlessly from grace. I am assured of this even more, because it is accompanied by a longing for inner silence. If I were you I would divide my outward pursuits in such a way that I could always follow the inclination of the spirit to silence and retirement. However, the constant quiet desire to renounce hustle and bustle does not harm work, it just helps to maintain focusing within, when we can't interrupt our outward pursuits.

You judge correctly the properties of your prayer, namely, that you let your head work too much. To stay constantly and fully silently accepting, is probably not useful to you, because of your character and capability; your doing should be more moderate, gentle and coming more from a child-like cordiality than from your head, this is without doubt. However may your predominant doing be to gaze at God and awaiting His actions in you, so that you surrender yourself completely to Him in all. Become like a child (Matthew 18:3) and think that you do not trust yourself in anything at all, but you entrust everything to the Father without the slightest embarrassment.

The rest at the meeting. Pray for me!

Müllheim, 31st December 1731

Dear brother!

I cordially greet you. God's Peace, as His Gift and the influence
of His presence is known by its fruits (Matt.7:20); and also by
the fact that among all the sorrows and trials it dwells in us
unshakably.

You ask how to behave so that our fallen state wouldn't disrupt it? The answer to this is not difficult: God's peace itself
is the best teacher. It leads us to simplicity, detachment from
everything that is not God and of God, inner freedom and purity. As soon as the soul begins to exalt itself even a little , or
manifest its ego in any other way, it will immediately fall into
devastation and confusion, and peace will abandon it. Therefore hold fast in a child-like manner and humbly to this peace,
whenever and in which way the Lord gives it to you, according to His grace given to you and reject anything that does not
correspond to it, immediately.

Encouraging spiritual feelings do not always and not neces-
sarily accompany God's peace; those may not be there, while
God's peace stays. To keep it to yourself, do not strain your
reason and feelings much, except perhaps out of necessity. Entrusting yourself and what is yours to the will of God should
be, as far as it is possible for you, complete. Then God's peace,
this the most quiet essence, will cause, inconspicuously and
gently, your soul incline more and more to God, making it a
true altar of His glory. I have to end the letter, because the
mail coach is waiting.

Commemorate before the Lord your feeble like-minded brother.

Müllheim, 3^d July 1737

Dear brother, cordially beloved in the Lord!

Obeying an inner impulse to greet you and to wish you God's peace with all my heart, I found time and opportunity to write you a few lines.

Let us give thought, dear brother, to what a great truth our Saviour has spoken: "In the world you will have difficulties." (John16:33). No matter how, wherever and whatever a person would be looking for, he will find nothing else. Our nature resists the cross and seeks to avoid it in every way, but will in no way escape it.

Generation after generation, paying no attention to the experience of their predecessors, will try to avoid the path of affliction, but will not be able to. It is impossible to have an easy and quiet life being part of the natural, fallen life. Christians, being sojourners and guests upon the earth (Heb.11:13), learn here humility and letting the former man die (Eph.4:22). In this dying, the way out of the torment and anguish of this world is revealed to them. And when they really begin to follow this way, they gain confident access (Eph. 3:12) to the promised land of rest and peace. This is the very God's peace, of which the Lord says: "...that you may have peace in me." (Jn.16:33); "Peace I leave for you; my Peace I give to you. Not in the way that the world gives, do I give to you." (John 14:27). And this peace is the best, the strongest and the only counterbalance to all suffering, sorrows and difficulties in our life here. Ah, Lord! And "who is against us?" (Rom.8:31), if You and Your deepest divine peace are with us? Even if the whole earth is in fear, wars, joylessness, nothing can harm us (Mark 16:18) if only we are "at peace with God, through our Lord Jesus Christ." (Rom. 5:1). But if it is not there in our hearts, then everything will torment us, from all sides. Oh, how I wish that every person would understand this!

When people hear that Christians are blessed, they think naturally that this means that in Christianity man can gain prosperity and avoid suffering. However it's not so.

Our damaged nature cannot and must not thrive; and our inner man cannot live unless he will leave behind our fallen nature, this world and our ego and all that is of it, for in all this there is no peace, but sorrow, sorrow and sorrow yet again.

Peace is only in Jesus. So let us "depart from their midst and be separate" (2 Cor. 6:17); let us surrender our fallen nature and our ego to the cross and let us be drawn by the guidance of love and peace into the wilderness of the spirit's detachment, in order to learn and to taste the elevated peace of God in Christ, which exceeds all understanding and which will guard our hearts and minds in Christ Jesus (Philippians 4:7). As for me, there is no other refuge and healing from every burden of this world, except, first of all, humility and acceptance of the will of God and, secondly, seeking peace in Jesus and preserving it through the distancing from everything that is not God and of God, and through focusing within.

May this hidden peace of Christ fill and strengthen our spirit in everything and at all times, so that God's work in us would continue unhindered until we accomplish our way in faith.

I stay your extremely feeble brother.

[Müllheim, presumably 1756–1763]

V. About the Childlikeness in Christ

In the grace of Jesus, our faithful Saviour, beloved friend and brother!

Your letter dated 4th August, in which you write about your sincere and renewed desire to belong entirely only the Lord, made me very happy. There's no need to ponder gravely what and how to write to me. We should be with one another like little children (Matt. 18:3) and come just to the point, then there will be no awkwardness. Truly the child-like mind of Christ (1 Cor. 2:16) does not look at objections of the fallen mind, which does not accept the ways of God, and pays no attention to those objections, but by placing itself into the presence of God silences the fallen reason.

Yes, the child is weak, short-sighted, often damages or breaks something. For this, the father admonishes or punishes him, but by no means banishes him from the house; he remains a beloved child. The child is sad in his heart that he upset his father; he promises to improve. This promise is quite infantile, but also sincere and comes from the heart. The father sees it and rejoices, although he well knows the weakness of his child.

It goes approximately the same way, dear brother, with our pursuits[6] and with our good inclinations and intentions. We must not estimate them too high or too low. A too high estimation is when we consider our decision to get down to work as the work itself, or when we are confident in ourselves that we can do things exactly the way we wanted to. A too low estimation is when we, initially confident that we can

6 By "pursuits" Tersteegen means here (and in similar passages) not only daily pursuits of every kind, including business but also works of piety (prayer, abstinence, certain ascetic practices, etc.)

do everything as it must be done, right on our own, cease doing anything at all, after being confronted with our existential incapability to realize this, and suppress our good intentions and motives with the imaginary pretext that we are not capable of anything at all. Undoubtedly we can do nothing on our own, but God can do everything, and our incapability encourages us to convert and to come to Him (John 15:5).

Any good feeling, intention, desire or thought does generate in us, but is God's working in us, which we must in no way reject or suppress in ourselves, but reverently accept and give it room in us. Also we must not think that God works good in us only initially, and then goes away and leaves us to ourselves, so that we will continue on our own. Not at all! Both at the moments when we discover good thoughts, desires or intentions in ourselves, and at all times, when we nourish and fulfill them, our Lord is inwardly close to us, bringing into action and preserving in us this good, as He is the true root and vine (Rev. 22:16; Jn. 15:5) of every good thing. It is He Who generates in us the desire for good and it is He Who realizes it in us, but "in accord with His own good will" (Phil. 2:13), and not according to what we think about it. Our concern should be staying cleanly within with God inside our heart, in all faithfulness to Him and steadfast hope in still new energy, which comes from our clinging to the vine (John 15:4), and letting Him act. When being confronted with our weakness and inconstancy, do not fall into faint-heartedness, but yet again go within to find new energy, because it can be found only there. O beloved brother! God is surely unspeakably close to us through the precious name of Jesus, in order to help us, to give us Himself, to love us and, in turn, to be reverently loved by us. He is our whole salvation and bliss! Let us draw near to Him; He is waiting for us, He reaches out, drawing us to Himself with His love. All this must be sought and found within, in the heart, and this can truly heal and save us already in this life, and to a much greater extent than it can be said. We need only to completely entrust ourselves to the Lord, love prayer and abiding within and not try to escape the bitterness of the crucifix. And this should be our utmost concern.

Before I received your letter, I had already written to N.N. everything necessary for his coming to his senses and edification. Why do children stumble and fall? Because they don't hold tight to their mother. Let this be a lesson and a warning to us!

I don't trust any great resolve unless this person diligently holds on to prayer and self-denial.

I greet you cordially and remain, in grace, your feeble and loving brother.

Letter 48. Enduring Suffering and inward Focusing onto God are the Way to the State of Childlikeness in Christ

"He learned obedience by the things that he suffered." (Heb. 5:8)

Beloved sister in the Lord!

Don't think that I forgot about you, no; I always remember the Lord! I heartily sympathize with your sorrows, which over-whelmed you both owing to your situation and your illness, and I wish you the Saviour's help and blessings , so that you would peacefully endure all the trials with benefit for your soul and obtain the spiritual fruit, which is true sanctifica-tion. Since God's grace brings forth the longing in you to ar-rive at the state of Christ's childlikeness (Matt. 18:3), then I, for my part, can only thank the Lord, Who instructs you on the path leading to this, no matter how strongly you fancy that it is not the case.

We become innocent children in Christ through the suffering and inner converting to God. The reason and the will of the former man (Eph.4:22) are completely opposite to this state of childlikeness. I can see that the goodness of God eradicates powerfully in you these two features of fallen state, which are so deeply nestled in us. He does it not so much through our bodily infirmities and headaches, but rather as the fact that the Lord does not let things go the way you would like neither around you nor inside you, but always in a different way (es-pecially in your current circumstances).

The time of suffering and adversity is the time of our fruit-ing, when we endure humbly and even joyfully calamities and hardships for the sake of the glorious fruit of obedience to

God. By this endurance we please Him more than by sacrifices, and it is this endurance which helps mainly in obtaining childlikeness in Christ.

Do everything that you can; and leave the rest to the Lord, Who will surely put all things together unto good (Rom.8:28). Reject everything that perplexes and confuses you and leads to cowardice. Pray to the Lord that everything that you do and what you endure is done for His sake. Stay with Him in your heart as long as you can; if you do not have the opportunity to be alone, then entrust this to the inner man and the love of God, which are not bound in any way. Therefore they can, even amidst the crowd and concerns cling to God inconspicuously and worship Him in spirit and in truth (John 4:24). May the Lord accomplish this by His grace and bless your soul forever!

Your feeble brother warmly welcomes you.

In the Lord Jesus Christ, may He live in your soul, beloved sister!

I've received your very kind letter to me dated September 8. Thank you for your benevolent concern! What is done for the Lord, is never lost, no matter how little it was. Our greatest accomplishments are nothing before the Lord; but a pure intention in God and a simple eye make everything significant and kind. People do not understand this; they look at what is being done, and not at the basis, from which the action comes. There's in the "great accomplishments" so much more of the fallen man, than of God, contrary to what is commonly thought. Man wants to serve God with, as he fancies them, grandiose and extraordinary accomplishments; but he would please God incomparably more in those small events and pursuits that Divine providence grants him right at the given moment.

Alchemists claim that even the simplest metals, like lead and iron, comprise some gold, and they try to extract it. And I say that in the tiniest and the most elementary things and actions there is something of God; and that's why, by accepting from God everything, enduring everything for the sake of God, and doing everything for God, man can make everything divine. This is the very art that I want to learn: to extract the true spiritual gold from everything. Little children in Christ (Matt.18:3) are the most capable of this. The Lord deprives them of the opportunity to accomplish great designs so that they would not be deceived by the outer brilliance, but more reliably and safely, in Christ's simplicity, follow such ways and do such works that seem small and insignificant, but which are dear to God and serve to His glorification. O! May the Lord inspire us with this in full measure, so that we may seek and find, not ourselves and our own, but Him alone in all and everything!

I greet you cordially in the spirit of love and remain your unanimous brother in Christ.

Müllheim, 13th October 1744

VI. On the Struggle against Sin. Spiritual Warfare

LETTER 53. ABOUT HOW TO LOOK AT YOUR SINS AND HOW TO
BEHAVE WHEN TEMPTED

In the grace of God, much beloved sister!

I received your kind letter last night and, not knowing when
another opportunity to send it to you will occur, I hasten to
write a short answer right away.
The fact that I have not been able to visit you lately, was of
course, God's tolerance. The aim of this is teaching you what I
have repeatedly drawn your attention to, namely: not to seek
and not to rely on people or any means. But seek and rely only
on God and His good will, and strive first of all to truly know
Him (1 John 5:20) and have communication with Him (1 Cor.
1:9). No creature can give you this. Meanwhile, I am quite surprised that you, showing many and various signs of trust in
me and in my words, now harbor absurd thoughts that I am
avoiding communication with you, because, as you think, of
your 'fallen and sinful nature'. I have repeatedly proved the
opposite and once again I assure you of this. Consider, then,
with certainty, that you need to be much simpler, not to reason so much and never to think badly about any person. <...>1
If you would understand several notions regarding sinfulness
and fall, and act according to them, your spiritual condition
would improve greatly.
These notions are as follows:
1) do not doubt that you are full of sinfulness;
2) do not love sin;
3) do not upset yourself because of your sinfulness;
4) do not think about sins. Then the door to sanctification
will soon be opened for you, and your soul will find rest.
1. Yes, there is even more sinfulness in you than you see now.
Yes, if it were not for the Lord and not for the action of His

grace, then anything that you do would be sinful. We believe and profess that we are fallen beings, but the facts of our lives seem to refute this. For whence comes that we despair and turn our face to the wall, when something improper manifests itself through us? Or, even more , when the Lord lets us painfully feel our deficiency and become fully aware of it through experience? As if we forgot that we carry a deposit of sins, but think that we have already advanced far on the path to God or that many virtues have become already rooted in us! Then it is God Who shows us that these fancied virtues are just selfishness and impurity. All our actions, because they are *ours*, are impure, (Job 14:4; Isaiah 64:4), even if they are done out of our pia desideria, meant to reach good goals. He who truly professes this will indispensably learn to refrain from selfwilled actions. As befits a Christian, surrender yourself fully to the Lord and humble yourself inwardly to such a degree that think of yourself as being not worthy of any comforting at all. More to it, be prepared to accept any kind of hardship given to you by God or by your fellowmen.

2. But though you are full of sinfulness, dislike sin! I mean this: when all the power of sin and evil surges up in you and you see everywhere nothing but temptations, then say with all your heart to God: "Lord! Despite everything, I don't want to sin." Gently, but resolutely deter your inner man from evil and turn heartily to the side of God, as strongly as you can. In Him and with Him no evil will harm you. If you cannot act like this at all, then humbly endure, like a rock that withstands the blows of a raging sea, or a tree, overwhelmed by hail and rain until the sun will shine again. When you see that your will bends favorably towards sin, then cry all the more with all your heart: "Lord! I don't want to sin!"

3. And do not be desolate because of your sinfulness. Perturbation and desolation, despair of the soul at temptations and seeing one's own fall prompts evil to become even more rag-

ing, and then instead of bearing and enduring temptation, we fall into actual sin. A restless and anxious heart is already half defeated and is not capable of bringing a good fruit. When the insidious serpent notices that the soul is afraid even of a slightest shadow, then it often terribly torments the soul, doing nothing but stealing the soul's time through this constant anxiety. Indeed, we would have reason to be afraid, to sigh, to worry, and to run God knows where, without looking back (as you write), if our Lord Jesus Christ had not been with us, who never leaves a sinner without His help. Although He allows our ship for some time to be flooded by waves, He doesn't manifest Himself (as it seems to us) (Mark 4:37).

Our impatient, untamed nature, damaged by the fall, does not want to wait, but to go right through, with fire and sword (Luke 9:54; John 18:10); it wants to be helped immediately, and if not, then it immediately despairs. No, dear soul! "act manfully; and let your heart be strengthened, and remain with the Lord." (Ps. 26(27):14).

4. Also do not think about sins, at least do not think intentionally. Thinking about them often gives rise to temptations. "Getting stuck" with your attention on your sins plunges you into cowardice and unbelief. Or perhaps are you scared that so many temptations will fall upon you and you will lapse in so many sins that Jesus can't help you? Oh unwise creature! Consider the sin and all that happens in you against your will, as if it were a matter that does not concern you at all. Drop all this abomination, it is unworthy of your attention and of your rummaging in it. Even if you feel the strongest uprise of sin in yourself, then try not to pay attention to this and rather let it vanish in oblivion. Experience will teach you that often great temptations are defeated by simply neglecting them. Have you nothing else to do in this life than to think all the time about sin? It is God and His presence that should be the main pursue of your heart. And if something else, either from out-

side or from the depth of your heart invades in it, then complain about it to God, even wordlessly, like a child and with all your heart. Exactly as you would say this to your best friend when he is with you. And hold on to Him alone, nothing else! Gaze at Him constantly with the eyes of your love (but do not think up images while gazing); worship Him in spirit and in truth in every place (John 4:23); revere Him. Surrender yourself to Him every moment; embrace Him in your heart. With other words: truly unite with Him and arrange your life entirely so that He is your most precious and faithful Friend and Father, and you are His child.

Pursue these and similar thoughts and feelings of the heart. Inwardly, adhere to them so that owing to them you forget about yourself, and the whole world, and sins. And if it comes to your mind: "Ah, I am worthless, fallen, full of sin, - answer yourself: "Yes, I know this, but I have no time to occupy myself with this."

Oh! If you could, like a child, follow this way Grace would sanctify you soon, even without your special efforts and philosophizing!

Before finishing this letter, which I do not want to make too lengthy, l want to answer your remarks, like e.g. "people are often angry with me", and further: "my relatives and friends shut themselves off from me", etc. Although I did not quite understand what you meant, I therefore will give you a general answer: perform your duties to the best of your ability as is necessary for the care of children and for housekeeping, with a humble and joyful disposition of the soul, and be sure that by doing so you serve and please the Lord greatly. Be friendly and compliant to everyone, and especially to your spouse in everything that does not go against God and your conscience, for it is the will of God (1 Pet. 3:1; Col. 3:18). If someone is angry with you in vain, then rejoice and think that the Saviour has been a stumbling block to many too. Should it be that something unkind breaks out of you unwillingly, in words or in deeds, so that your fellow-men are justly angry with you, then humble yourself in your heart before God. And if the circumstances require then admit sincerely to people your wrong. But just don't upset yourself because of this and don't worry too much so that the last won't be worse than the first. On the contrary, rather give yourself over to grace, so that it will strengthen and comfort you. The race of God is like a mother, quickly picking up her child who fell into the mud. Therefore turn to Grace instead of staring at the mess you're in.

I know you will find something to object to in this letter of mine; however I have answered those objections more than once before, and besides my head is so weak at the moment that writing wearies me. I do not pretend at all to teach you or whoever it may be, because I myself am full of darkness and fallen nature. Just as a simpleton I follow your desire and I think that this letter will give you some consolation. I've been away for a few days and, maybe I'll leave soon, so I don't know when God will allow us to "speak face to face". (2 John 1:12).

Pray for me! I hope the Lord will also bless me to pray for you. I cordially greet you, as well as your spouse. Faithful is the God who calls us (1 Thess. 5:24); He will not abandon you (Heb. 13:5).

In Him I remain your benevolent friend and fellow wanderer in this world.

Müllheim, 10th October 1729
(Abbreviated)

Beloved sister in the grace of the Lord Jesus!

I can see from your letter that my last message to you has been of great benefit to you.

It makes me very happy; not because I wrote it, but because I set out in it, as far as in me lies, divine truths. They are beneficent and redeeming for all of us, and especially for you. May God strengthen you in His truth, and grant you to come into a child-like state of which Christ spoke (Matt. 18:3). Then in time you will come to know His miracles much better than any description of them in words can tell you.

I often think with great compassion of those Christians, who, being in many ways very faithful to God, day after day and year after year torment themselves with many useless great efforts and cause great anxiety to themselves. This is because they do not know the remedy that could easily help them, namely: to abide within their hearts, quietly and in child-like innocence with Jesus and in Jesus, Who is so close to us. Oh! Those toiling and burdened with this ignorance! Come and turn with confidence, as children, inwardly to Christ, and you will find rest for your souls! (Matthew 11:28-29; 18:3).

However what was said above no one will understand properly, until the hour comes and the Lord reveals it to the soul. Thank Him then that He has granted you to see this way and to taste it somehow. Preserve this grace in the silence of your heart, do not talk much about it, for most people are incapable of listening to this (Heb. 5:11). Also because of the novelty of the light that has dawned on you do not give too much room to the movements of your feelings; carefully cover this fire, so that it would burn quietly, but constantly. As for the resisting and rebellion of your fallen nature and reason, this is not at all surprising.

They [fallen nature and reason] are used to being the main advisers of the soul and believe that in everything that the soul does it should listen to them and give them an account. Send them all back and let them murmur there. Children don't philosophize, they trust their mother unconditionally. Days come, within us and outside of us, when every human wisdom will be confounded before the child-like spirit of a Christian! Yes, amen!

Answering your discourse about with what you should keep yourself busy: with your sinfulness or with the love of God in Jesus Christ? It is very important for a neophyte to explore his/her inner and outer disposition; his/her words, deeds, thoughts and desires in order to see clearly his/her sins and damaged, fallen nature, so that the self-knowledge and fear of God of the soul would grow. It is therefore very good and useful to learn this. However, this work cannot bring anyone to perfection, righteousness and holiness; it only brings him/her to a better hope (Heb. 7:19). The best hope, best way, best work consists of this: by faith, trusting in the blood of Jesus Christ that cleanses us (Hebrew 9:14), approach God with childlike simplicity (as Paul calls on in Hebrews 7:19) and enter into the closest fellowship with Him in your heart. I believe that especially for you it will be many times more useful and edifying than "getting stuck" on your sins, as I have told you more than once.

How can it be displeasing to God when you, in order to think about Him and abide with Him, forget yourself with all your "great sinfulness"? Moreover, you know well that you cannot help yourself in anything; only He, your Saviour can help you. And in vain you are afraid that with Him you will learn about yourself and your [primordial] damage to a lesser extent, than when you scrupulously examine yourself and rummage about in your sins. On the contrary, you will see your fall and your ego in a much more efficient manner and much more precisely, without making special efforts to this, - namely, in the true light of God and in His presence. In this case, awareness of your sins humbles you, but it does not disrupt you and does not plunge you into cowardice and despondency. The Christian therefore does not get bogged down in sins, but, as it were, moves away from them into the depth, immersing in the sweetest love of the Lord Jesus. The Lord wants us to fully trust Him, and come to Him like children (Matt. 18:3), no matter how pathetic we are. For this is His merciful willingness to live and act in us and make us truly His loved ones (Eph. 2:19). And let the fallen reason stumble over love of mankind and condescension of our God and regard it as foolishness (1 Cor. 2:14): we will not let false humility get in the way of the glory of God and our good!

Finally, try inwardly more and more to be like a child with God in the depths of your soul. When you feel a child-like reverence for God's -presence, quiet well-being, the impulse of love to focusing within and heartfelt silence and the like, then believe that your divine Friend wants to visit you. Give Him room, as much as you can, and humbly follow His actions. Quieten and restrain your feelings, thoughts, will, and any self-willed action. Such suppression of the activity is by no means idleness (as you write). Let all the images before your inner eye and all human implications scatter in the presence of God! He is incomprehensible. Just believe that He is present with you! It refers to your inner state; if you manage to preserve it during your everyday activities, then everything outside you will be good and pleasing to God.

You see, I wanted to write you just a few lines, but it became very many lines, about so important truths. May God reveal them to us, and may He lead us into them!

The books you've mentioned are good; but don't read much now. Do not distract yourself by reading; you need to read a little and only that, which can contribute to your focusing within. So turn to God, come to God, but not to me; say a prayer for my soul, and after this forget me and all that is mine.

Henceforth, when you write to me, do not address me with elevated titles, but just as your friend, as I hope to remain, by the grace of the Lord Jesus Christ.

Müllheim, 11th February 1730

LETTER 55. ABOUT THE PRESENCE OF GOD. ABOUT ONE'S AWARENESS OF THE SIN AND EGO IN ONESELF

Heartily beloved brother in the grace of the Lord Jesus!

You write to me about your state of mind. I certainly see in it the hand of God which guides you; so you don't have to worry. Without proper experience, it is impossible to believe that there can co-exist in a soul at the same time two opposites: grace and sin[7]; but in fact it is the Lord Who arranges it so. The grace of God is the light that allows us to see all the darkness of sin and ego (Eph. 5:13). When this happens, the Lord wisely draws away from us His presence, otherwise our feeble being would die being not able to bear the purity of God. But since He desires to heal us, He proportions His actions to the capacity of the soul. Give thanks to God, that He makes you aware of His presence; thank Him also for exposing to you the darkness of your fallen nature, which can be seen only in His light. Endure the afflictions which are caused by this granted awareness with humility and surrender all [of you] to His will, so that the flame of His love would burn down your ego; this is however still a long way off.

On the one hand, you partly see your fallen nature, image, which is truly the image of a serpent and the tree of self-love with countless big and small branches; the axe must cut this tree to the root (Matthew 3:10). On the other hand, your spirit partly feels that God is infinitely good, that He is present

7 This refers not to a deliberately committed sin, but to the general sinfulness, the fallen nature of man. Compare it to the words of St. Makarios the Great: "Often grace acts in man incessantly, just as the eye in the body. But at the same time there dwells in man sin too, and leads the mind into delusion. Word 1, § 11.

with us, and that in His inner presence our life becomes more abundant (John 10:10) and we find supreme joy and contentment.

Our spirit wants to be there, although the lower, outer part of our being has a completely different predisposition. Separation of these parts is by no means completed in you (Heb. 4:12), although it seems that each part lives for itself and is at enmity with the other. Sometimes the inner man comes out too much; sometimes he is so attracted by God's presence to immerse in Him, that he almost does not see the outer [world] at all. However you can help your inner man in no other way than by enduring, when possible in a receptive manner, [patiently], without getting involved in anything external, everything that happens to you (Luke 21:19): when evil - then candidly, in simplicity not accepting it and not consenting to it; when good, and every action of God - approving them and surrendering yourself to God.

Just be peaceful! Everything will be fine, even if tribulations multiply. God wants you to be completely His, no matter how the life of self-love is horrified. Finishing the letter I entrust you to the care of the Lord so close to us and remain your devoted brother.

Müllheim, 27th August 1734

VII. On the Cross and Suffering

LETTER 74. AN EXHORTATION NOT TO DESCEND FROM THE CROSS. IN THE CRUCIBLE OF SUFFERING WE LEARN TO SUFFER AND THE TESTER (JER. 6:27) IS OUR FRIEND. HOW TO BEHAVE WHEN TEMPTED BY OUR NEIGHBOUR

Beloved brother in the Lord!

Truly, I behold your state and your illness, on the one hand, with brotherly sympathy, on the other hand, with reverence for the wise and redeeming ways of the Lord. What should I say to you? In any case, "don't descend from the cross" (Matt. 27:40); on the contrary, endure it as much as you can, peacefully and with hope on God. This is His way; the Lord's hand is there and invisibly supports you. "In a little while, and somewhat longer, he who is to come will return, and he will not delay. (Heb.10:37). Our neophyte's idea of Christianity is crippled: we often forget about the true Path of the Cross (Philippians 3:18). Yes, we are ready to participate in Christ's suffering (1 Pet. 4:13), but as heroes. Our suffering should be elevated, worthy, seeing and praised by all, clear and understandable, not unexpected and not at all painful.

We want to bear the cross, but only not the one that is given to us. We do not mind enduring all sorts of sorrows, with the exception of those that we have. In short: actually we do not want to suffer or endure; it seems to us unbearable at once.

Take heart, my brother! You have to learn to suffer and it is done through suffering; and when you've learned it, then the spirit tastes the sweet fruit, which emerged from a bitter root. O! pure, sweet and peaceful, most inner tasting of the Spirit, which is born from the cross and suffering and which is less easily damaged by selfishness than the other gifts of God! And although a Christian who undergoes this training dwells in such darkness, that he does not see the preciousness of suffering and its fruit, the Lord, when necessary, touches him, and opens his eyes for a short while, strengthening and soothing him. Sometimes He even raises him completely above views and feelings of the fallen nature.

I am asking you to let the all-good and all-wise God treat you as He pleases! Don't explore His ways and your sorrows with your reason; accept them and serve the Lord as He determines, and not you, and in that position and the state in which you are. This is precisely what will serve your spiritual growth and bring you peace. Your past views on the way of salvation were not wrong; however everything takes root and ripens through the cross.

The concepts you have compiled, of course are not always in accordance with this; but the very matter of salvation is in no way affected by this, but goes forth as it should, and incomparably higher and deeper than we understand the words of the promises of salvation.

The beautiful land of Canaan was promised, and Israel went out of Egypt with hope (Ex. 6:4). Meanwhile many found death in the wilderness (Num. 16:33), and Israel's hope was to undergo great trials (Num. 21:4); a long time passed. But God keeps His word, and children born in the wilderness inherited the land flowing with milk and honey (Ps. 69:36-37). The Messiah and His kingdom were promised long ago, expected and most solemnly shown in signs. The Messiah has come, but like a poor baby. His disciples thought differently about His Kingdom: sometimes it seemed to them that there was no longer any hope for it to come (Matt. 26:56); then wait, it will be coming ... (Acts 1:6). His Kingdom did come, but it was quite different from their coarse earthly notions. Christ's Kingdom is not of this world (John 18:36), and it came to the disciples inwardly, through their salvatory experience of the Lord's reign in their hearts (Luke 17:21; Acts 2:3). This reign brings such peace, divine majesty and glory, compared to which all the kingdoms of this world are only a lifeless and miserable dream.

Therefore, I urge you once again, my brother: be of good cheer (Jn.16:33) and do not fall away (Luke 8:13). Give yourself completely to the Lord without sparing your fallen nature and ego, and trusting that He knows best how, when and where to uproot them from you. You do not suffer alone (1 Pet. 5:9), and I am with you with all my heart.

P.S. Precisely when I wanted to seal this letter there came another one from you, from two days ago. I add a short answer to it too. Write to me without hesitation or embarrassment as soon as the need arises. All your letters please me, though I cannot always answer them with a pen. But in God's grace through them we embrace each other in spirit, that already is a great good, even if we do not receive any other benefit.

Don't be fainthearted, or at least endure your faint-heartedness as peacefully as you can. I assure you that there is in your present state no danger. It is just that you do not see the hand that guides you and protects you. Gold should be cleansed; cleansing fire causes suffering and sorrow; man does not see gold, but only impurity; the spirit, or the highest part of our being, is completely concealed by soot. Such is our fate.

We have to go through all this, understand and deeply feel it, and drink to the end this most bitter cup for our pride. We try to get rid of it, but doing this we sink even more into dross and filth. If it were not for the indelible thirst within us for God and His pure life, then this process would be completely unbearable for us. But the Tester (Jer. 6:27) was, is, and remains our Friend. He sees and He knows how long this process must last and how far it must reach. And thus the Christian learns to entrust himself exclusively to grace and learns the need of a completely new life in Christ; learns to accept this new life and obey it. Here he finally says goodbye to the fallen reason and unconditionally confesses before God and people: I am receiving what my deeds deserve (Luke 23:41), even if he does not see himself guilty of anything.

Further you ask: would it not be better to explain yourself to brother N., who (as you write) hurts you. Answer: yes, it is better as N. for such a long time annoys you and you can no longer bear it. Besides you have reason to be sure that N., having learned about your discontent, will willingly meet you halfway and stop doing what he did out of ignorance. In that case, in my opinion, it will be good if you will humbly talk it all out. And not so much for you to get relief, but to uproot the bitter root of a greater evil, that is hostility between friends, so that your brother wouldn't be upset, seeing you suffer and not knowing how to help you, because you shut yourself to him.

However, it will be endless talk if we would try to reveal to our neighbor all that plagues us or annoys us in them, in what we imagine about them. Likewise when we imagine our does something wrong (whether only in our imagination or in reality and tell him/her, there will be no end to the discussion. Often such a discussion about one or another trifle causes much trouble.

For the urge of discontent comes from inside, and not outside of us; and when it seizes the soul, everything annoys us, so that when we would eliminate one annoyance, then it is immediately replaced by two others. Therefore, the best way is just to endure most of such temptations; then as a rule they disappear without being discussed and we see what has happened in a different light. I have no doubt that Brother N. does not make you feel bad intentionally, although you see it precisely so. In fact, when God wants to try and to teach us and He imposes on us for this purpose some kind of sorrow, then often our neighbor, though completely unwillingly, speaks to us or acts in such a way that we suffer greatly from this.

And sometimes it is the tempter who stirs up all sorts of trifles and insignificant things in our clouded imagination. Speaking generally: I'm asking you, when such a dark cloud comes upon you, do not try too much to dispel it because you might get annoyed even more. Acknowledge your weakness, the fact that your nature is fallen, and your nothingness and immerse yourself, when possible, in the pure grace of God, patiently waiting for help from the Lord (Ps. 121:2); this will be more than enough.

The hour of the Lord will come, and deliverance will come. Jesus is with you, my brother!

Müllheim, 18th December 18, 1749

LETTER 93. TO A CERTAIN MERCHANT (PROBABLY TO ADRIAAN PAUW. TRANSLATORS) ABOUT NOT GIVING UP YOUR TRADING BUSINESS. AN EXHORTATION TO FOLLOW THE INNER CALL OF GOD. PRACTICAL ADVICE. WHAT JESUS SAYS TO US

In the grace of the Lord Jesus much beloved brother.

I received both of your letters on time, but for many reasons I could not write back sooner than today, though I have answered you in the spirit. May the Lord strengthen us, and may He withdraw by His love the strivings of our hearts from all the external goals, and direct them to Himself, so that we may become one soul and one heart in Him! (Acts 4:32). Amen.

As for your trading business, I will repeat the humble advice I gave you in my last letter, that you do not yet abandon it. Continue in it as it goes on, and see it as an exercise in self-lessness, patience and faith, for I believe that your spirit does not yet have such a strength in God that you can completely renounce earthly things. I therefore consider the pursuits of your outer man, done with trust in God's providence and in self-denial, to be much less dangerous for you than it would be when you would follow a contemplative way of life and failed to withstand the inner temptations that come with it. In the meantime try as far as possible to arrange and limit your outward pursuits so that they would not weigh down your spirit too much and so that you may always have some time for solitude and focusing within.
I say "as far as possible" because I know very well that the trading business is not very conducive to this. There are always occasions for temptation, now through disbelief, now through love for money.

Such occasions should not dismay us or drive us into despondency; on the contrary, they ought to encourage us to deny ourselves and all other supports so that our spirit may hunger and thirst for Him alone and cling to Him alone, Who keeps us when we pass through the waters and walk through fire(Isaiah 43:2). There is no support anywhere but only and solely in God, Whom we truly find when we are stripped of self-support and any other support but Him.

This way is little understood, but its end is glorious. Oh, how poor and oh, how rich will be our spirit, having nothing but God! Oh, Lord, let this be fulfilled in us!

Of course, dear brother, it takes a lot, as you write, to love God without self-interest or selfishness. But it is so that this "a lot" is not obtained suddenly, all at once. It is necessary to surrender to the guidance of God right at *this moment* and fully to the extent that man is aware of at *this moment*. And God, who has begun this good work in us, will Himself perfect it (Philippians 1:6). If man finds [by surrendering himself to the guidance of God] only himself, then that is also grace; then he should lose himself in God again there where he found himself.

For there can be no true self-denial if we do not first find and feel ourselves all the way through[8].

The main thing is to follow the good attraction and call (John 6:44; 10:3), with which God touches our spirit with His love and awakens in us deep thirst and desire to abandon ourselves and fallen creation and unite with Him, with the Source of our life. Let the looking forward to this attraction and call of God and surrendering ourselves to them (whether in the nakedness of faith or in our mind and feelings) be that "yet only thing" which is necessary (Luke 10:42). As for our mind and feelings, here you need to know that there act in our feelings and thoughts now good, then evil forces. Then the sun

---

8 See ourselves as we really are.

shines in them, and then the person is cheerful, fresh, fiery; then the influence of evil enters into them, and a person, in the same degree to which a moment before he was pious and fiery, becomes dead and powerless. Therefore he who desires stability, let him not linger on the sphere of thoughts and feelings, but let him, in his spirit [and faith], immerse himself in God and cling to Him; this is the only true way to salvation.

I can easily imagine that in your present state, life constantly gives you lessons and takes you through trials. Always cast everything like that before God and don't bear it for long inside. Excessive thinking in such cases does not help, but only confuses and spoils everything. And more to it: our bodily infirmities render us a constant occasion to constantly have our souls in our hands (Ps. 118:109), that is, to be ready for the departure and not to look too much at the outer matters. A heartfelt entrusting of oneself and one's children to the Lord is undoubtedly the best thing to do when you think about the future. However it will be by no means superfluous for the sake of your and your family's peace to make a formal will. Only include in it as the executor and manager thereof, in addition to your relatives, a third party, namely, a skillful friend who is favorably disposed towards you and would keep everything in his hands and oversee that everything would happen in due order. Such was the thought which crossed my mind; however, I am becoming more and more like a baby in worldly matters.

<...> Your brotherly proposal to move in with you, I perceive as evidence of your sincere love, which I hope to always reciprocate. But God's will keeps me in my place; besides, the few days left to me to live, do not allow me to think about moving, changing and other worries. May God bless that we live in unity with each other in the heart of Jesus here and in eternity! Amen.

I must finish my letter, dear brother, for my head won't let me write anymore; it is already several days I feel worse again. I greet and embrace you in the spirit together with all and each of you who strive to be a child of God; I do not mention the names, so as not to offend anyone whose name I would omit because I do not remember it anymore. I remember often all of you, and I rejoice together with you, share your meal of love in spirit. May God bless N. and give her grace to understand His admonitions properly. With all her Martha's external pursuits, may her inner being become Mary, who sits at the feet of Jesus listening to His word. The entire variety of life must come together into this one act(Luke 10:39, 41). Jesus speaks His word through those works of grace in our hearts which instruct and inspire us (1 John 2:27). His words also resound through divine providence in every deed, event and matter, which we meet in the daily course of life. And all these Our Lord's utterances aim at this one thing: that we truly die to ourselves (John 12:24) and become "transferred" into His divine life and into inner communion with Him. Only in this we find eternal life (1 John 5:20).

Your soul mate desires from his heart that the Lord may give N. and all of us to come to know this in our essence.

Müllheim, 27th January 1736
(Abbreviated)

VIII. About the Life of God in us

In the name of Jesus. Beloved brother!

Since I have the opportunity to send you a letter, I greet you and all yours with love of my heart and I wish you to learn still deeper and purer the fullness of the good given to us in Jesus Christ by glorifying His mercy to us which we do not deserve! We know, dear brother, that we need only Jesus, and that for our sanctification and salvation we must truly live only for Him. So let us give Him a room in us to act and let us completely entrust everything that concerns us to Him! He Himself will willingly help us in this. He is present in us; He is closer to us than we are to ourselves. He does everything to pour in us His divine life and Himself. He undoubtedly assures us with so many precious manifestations of His grace to attract us. Oh! If we just won't show ourselves unworthy of this, answering Him with distraction and unfaithfulness! No matter how weak are the hidden manifestations of the pure life of Jesus in us. We can always feel its, even small, movements and if we give it a room in us, it weakens the intensity of life of our fallen feelings, reason and ego.

Oh! If we only would endeavor by means of the works of faith, focusing within ourselves and quietening of the soul (as far as it is in our power), to discern more and more precisely in ourselves those actions of life of Jesus. And consider committing ourselves to this life as our primary pursuit!

It is our disbelief that makes us think that the Lord will not let us experience that, what the Apostle Paul once testified of himself, to the glory of the grace of God: "I live; yet now, it is not I, but truly Christ, who lives in me." (Gal. 2:20).

Oh, how disgusting is the life of the fallen ego! And how beautiful and gracious is the life of Jesus, which hunts down the life of the ego anywhere and everywhere, up to its complete and redeeming death! Oh, Jesus! Only he can say: "I live" in whom only You live, for You are "true God, and…Eternal Life" (1 John 5:20).

To Him, my beloved brother, I entrust your heart as well as those of all my friends around you (I will not list them by name). Remember me too before the Lord. To Him be glory forever!

LETTER 98. THE DIFFERENCE BETWEEN TRUE AND FALSE INNER SILENCE AND INACTIVITY

Beloved brother and friend!

I just received your letter and I want to answer though briefly, but immediately, because it is already late in the evening, and tomorrow morning I intend to leave.
From your letter I learned about the extreme bodily weakness, which was the Lord's visit to you. I sympathize with you very much and I hope that the Lord will give you the necessary strength and relief (1 Cor. 10:13). It's great that your spirit is peaceful, this is undoubtedly the grace of God. Unity of our inner man with God and accepting all His ways which He sets out for us is the best and easiest remedy to imperturbable peace of mind. But if these ways of God are opposing the will of the fallen nature, and it rebels and makes its dissatisfaction felt for us, then it won't be even a slightest problem for us. Periods of sorrow and suffering are the times of our testing and learning.
I will answer your doubts in a nutshell. There are many types of inner silence and inactivity[9], and you need to know clearly the difference between their true and false manifestations.

---

9 The word "inactivity" is the translation of the term Gelassenheit (lit. "leaving", "letting go"), which is important for a pietist's spirituality. It means "receptive surrender to God." In the 18th century the understanding of this term began to shift towards the "apathy" of the Stoics, that is, freedom of soul from passions and affections, but "autonomous-human", without God. Tersteegen argued tirelessly against such a "godless" perception of the ascetic "surrendering oneself". In a similar manner Christian "Gelassenheit" differs from Taoist "non-action".)

When a man, who is not mortified in regard to the old Adam, and whose will, consciousness and love therefore are actually still dominated by sin or inclined towards sin and dominated by or inclined towards what is created, and not by God[Creator] throws up his hands and lets everything go as it goes, then this is a false inactivity. When such a man, fancying to comply with the notion of piety, strives to focus forcing his thoughts and feelings and finds inner silence, then such silence and such passionlessness would be false.

Contrary to the above is when a sincere soul strives for its inner being to truly rid itself from everything that is not God or of God, realizing at the same time the impossibility of riding itself on its own from being captured by sin and ego. When it longs with all its heart to be of God right now, not someday, and for this, it surrenders all of itself to God and His actions. Such a soul desires willingly to endure the hardships of the upbringing of the Spirit, no matter what inner and outer suffering it may cost. Such a soul need not worry whether it is trapped in false silence and inactivity. It is such a soul which should restrain itself from actions of its fallen reason and feelings, because this would be unfaithfulness towards God. The self-willed actions of the soul do not leave room for God's actions and therefore the soul gets trapped in the maze of its self-will.

Our only work should be, while renouncing ourselves (Matt. 16:24) and the fallen creation (1 John 2:15), to put on the pure love of God (Col.3:14). It is done by turning inward in a humble surrender of oneself and all what one is and has, to God, even if we are not always exactly aware of what this is (it is also not necessary). Man experiences the above described going on within and surrenders as follows: his/her heart sincerely averts from all that is created; his/her will in everything is tuned according to what pleases God; the eye of the soul in child-like simplicity gazes only at God, Whom alone he/she wants to know; his/her love accepts and embraces the inwardly present Good as that which makes up the fullness of his/her life; etc.

All this, I say, is accomplished in Christ (Matthew 18:3) by the childlike work of going within oneself and humbly surrendering to God. Such work often becomes so spiritual and simple, so far away from sensuality and self-will, that it can no longer be called work. It is then true stillness and inactivity, and this is the best of all. Since it is done by the heart and spirit, and not by head and feelings, then through the latter all sorts of dispelling thoughts, temptations, cloudiness, and sometimes unclean things come, against one's will, when one's soul does not even want to accept anything like that. The soul however need not worry in such a case, because it is not in its power to deal with such intrusions; on the contrary, the efforts of the soul will only make the situation worse. The soul should not consent in the heart to those intrusions and abide inwardly in stillness, equanimity and trust in God.

For the enemy tries most to confuse the soul and "drag it out" from within through all kinds of fears, worries, doubts, confusing thoughts and other temptations. Not infrequently the Lord allows this in order to teach the soul and strengthen the 'hidden person of the heart' (1 Pet. 3:4). For surely before we establish ourselves on our inner path, we have to go through many inner and outer battles and doubts. However, simplicity in Christ helps avoid many dangers.

It's time to finish the letter, there is no time left at all. I write quickly, in a simple way, and in a hurry I might not express myself clearly enough; but you know all this much better than me. Let God bless us in Jesus and give us understanding.

I cordially greet you, along with all yours. Let the Lord turn our love away from everything and draw it to Himself, and let our suffering help this too! I remain your feeble fellow-wanderer in this world.

Beloved sister in the Lord Jesus Christ!

I've received your kind letter in a timely manner. Reading it
made my heart joyful. My bodily weakness and excessive labor are the only reasons why I didn't answer it right away. I
thank God from the bottom of my heart, that His eternal love
touches and draws you, so that you live wholly for Him and
for eternity, following Him on the way of focusing within and
prayer of the heart. O! It's more reliable and the most child-
like blissful path, the only one on which our spirit is freed
from all the ties that bind it and ascends into real peace!
Our sojourn on earth is to us a hard, wretched and alien
life; we only wander through it (Heb.11:13). God is our true
Father, and quiet eternity is our true homeland; we are at
home there. We would never have found this homeland (Heb.
11:14), if God had not sent His only begotten Son (1 John 4:9),
so that He may come to seek and save the lost (Matt. 18:11).
Through the sweetest name of Jesus God becomes intimately
close to us in our hearts. He makes this world bitter for us
and everything outside the Lord, loathsome.
He gives rise in us to a thirst for Him and aspiration in the
heart to communion and unity with Him. He satisfies this
thirst and aspiration by giving us from time to time, which
is totally not according to our merits, to partake of His goodness and peace, so that draws us to Him and strengthens us in
bearing our cross and in self-renunciation. O! How merciful
the Lord is to poor sinners, who draw near to Him! (James
4:8).
Therefore, dear sister, think not of deceit or danger: surely
it comes from God that at times you find in yourself a deep

silence, peace and well-being, not knowing where it comes from and where it is going (John 3:8). It is a kind of "universality" or wholeness of true prayer, containing all the particular wishes, which we usually offer up to God when praying to Him. Our feelings actions, thoughts, pious zeal, etc., may touch the soul, not for long, and through prayer to delight the outer man. However that which subsides and brings content to the very foundation of our heart only God can give by His drawing nearer and His presence. Hence it happens that you not often abide in that state. If it were in your power to generate such a peace and well-being in you on your own, then you would nourish yourself by them without ceasing. Also the soul in this state has no doubt that it was God Who drew nearer to it. But when you go back to yourself and to the work of reasoning and feelings, then, since the soul does not get much from them, doubts are inevitable.

False freedom or false lack of anxiousness consists in the fact that a person, allegedly refusing "pseudo-spirituality" and "self-willed action", is actually guided by his/her ego and negligence for prayer. Such a person, being still in every possible way committed to the world, to the fallen creation and to his/her fallen nature, and having no notion of what is God's action and God's drawing nearer, just doesn't want to do at least something to come to know this. The Divine freedom and lack of anxiousness come together with the deepest reverence for God's presence and experience of peace and well-being, which I have mentioned before and which cannot be granted to man by anything in this world. Even though the soul does not always feel and notice those subtle manifestations of God as they are, it certainly sees the fruit of this divinely silent prayer: a person's inclination to withdraw from the created; longing for God and for the eternal; heartfelt desire to please God; quietening and pacifying of all manifestations of the soul etc. In a word: through this focusing within and silence,

God's presence acts in us and the life of Jesus is poured in us, which gradually encompasses our heart.

It does not surprise me at all that you complain about the absentmindedness and weakness that come upon you when you come to your outer pursuits, and that you repeat so easily the same mistakes. Your inner life is like a seed so far, not yet a fruit; but this is a seed that contains the great tree (Matt. 13:31–32), noble seed, elevated vocation, great grace!

Cultivate it in the silent focusing within, tend it with great devotion and value this precious pearl (Matt. 13:46) above all! Our mistakes and infirmities should serve to increasing our humility, but not to make us cowards. Do not believe your ego, but trust God endlessly. Love holy solitude, but do not abandon the works required of you by the course of events, love or obedience; do them like a child who fulfills the will of his father.

Just write to me as soon as the need arises, although due to my weakness and being busy, I cannot always reply.

I always remember you with love before the Lord; and you also pray for me. I cordially greet you and remain, by grace, your sincerely devoted to you feeble brother.

Müllheim, 1757

LETTER 103. THAT GOD'S ACTION IN THE HEART SHOULD NOT
BE OBSCURED BY REASON. PROPERTIES OF THE GRACEFUL
DRAWING BY GOD

Dear brother!

As far as your state of mind is concerned the best and safest
course of action would be for you to try to calmly endure everything, that resists God's drawing (John 6:44) in the heart
and your good spirit. Keep yourself in such disposition, as
firmly as you can, without fear and guesses, and don't get
distracted by something else. Drawing by grace and God's
light do not come from outside. They receive their fullness
(1 Thessalonians 1:5) and strength not from our reason and
feelings. They abide in the depths of the heart and by themselves possess great persuasiveness and reliability. Their reliability, however, becomes obscured and disappears when the
soul wants to acquire certainty and confidence in its lower
part[10]. Therefore don't immerse in thinking too much. Don't
try to establish yourself in the spirit with the help of rational conclusions alone or external means. Close your eyes and
surrender yourself like a child, to that hidden God (Isaiah
45:15), Who is so close to us inwardly; and let the mind doubt
as much as it pleases. We would have given to the mind, and
next to it, to the tempter too much credit if we would start
arguing with them. Let us look for our reasons and argu-
ments not at them, but in the light of faith revealed to us in
the depths of our heart. At first, the drawing of God to the
inner life is gratifying and delightful: a person rejoices, sincerely follows the call of God, etc. The lower part of the soul,
in which all this is reflected in some way, does not object to
this at all (or nearly at all). But later on [God's] grace immers-

---

10 In the mind and feelings (emotions).

es deeper, in the inner, or higher, part of our being. Then the lower part begins to resist and show its displeasure, because it remains without sweets, and besides, it is also fueled by the tempter. Then many changes happen to a person, shocks and even troubles; these are all to confuse him and distract him from the goal. You can oppose this by resorting to a childlike simplicity in Christ (Matt. 18:3) and be content only with the secret light of faith in the heart. Therefore stay, as far as the grace of God gives you, in the focusing within and receptiveness and be peaceful and content with what happens to you according to the will of God, for it is good, pleasing and perfect (Rom. 12:2) everywhere and always, and in relation to us too.

I prayerfully entrust your condition to God's care and ask also your prayers, for I am very weak.

Müllheim, 23ᵈ February 1733

Most precious sister in the sweetest love of Jesus!

I received both of your letters, the previous one, through Mr
N., and the current letter from Frankfurt, in good order and
read them with joy; Glory to God!
Of course, I should have answered earlier. But it would take
too long to describe the reasons why I could to do this only
today; may love explain everything to you in the best way!
When I received your first letter, I just, at the insistent desire
of friends, was preparing for a trip to Holland. There are there,
among many "outward" and, so to speak, "mixed" Christians
still some "inward" hearts, who seek to follow the path of dying of the former man (Eph.4:22) and the life in God in fullness. I was so sick there that I thought that my end was coming. The Lord however ruled that later I felt much better and
I was able, accompanied by a friend of mine to return home.
Since then, I've been getting better and then again everything
worsened to an extreme degree so that my life's energy was
exhausted and I thought that the end of my earthly journey
had come. So, being pressed from all sides, I was compelled to
keep my soul continually in my hands (Ps. 119:109) and truly
become a sojourner and guest on earth (Heb. 11:13).
Lonely, estranged from everything which is transient and resorting to God only. Trusting only in the notion that the good
Lord, Who draws us to Him because of His free love, filling
us with longing and thirst for heaven, Himself will bring me
there. Undoubtedly, it is exactly His divine presence and the
action of His Spirit in us, that we have in our spirit so deeply
imprinted the thirst and striving to emerge from the fallen

creation and ego and be found in God (Philippians 3:9), our true life and unshakable joy!

God's love touches us at the base of our heart; for our part, we do not need to act here much from ourselves. If we only child-like stay inside, detach ourselves from everything that is not God and of God, and /accept this love of His, then it becomes our worker. Its meek and quiet power draws us out of ourselves to that depth where we belong, although this is not always known to us explicitly.

The Lord gradually takes away from the soul every external aid and support and the soul's hope on itself, so that He alone, in purity, becomes all of this. When this happens to us, we mustn't become afraid; it is the act of His love. He who wants to keep everything in his hands and thus save his soul (Mk. 8:35), always lives in narrowness and difficulties. When we, so to speak, with our eyes closed, completely and unconditionally surrender ourselves to God, then we are gradually introduced into the joy of freedom and vastness of spirit, where the love of God does for us everything that would be impossible for us, and leads us there where it wants us to be (John 14:23; 17:24). Let's become, beloved sister, wholly of God; let's perceive our souls as things handed over to the Lord Jesus, about which we no longer have to worry. He will free and save them, as He sees fit; we only have to allow Him to act. To love and glorify Him is our work, that we fulfill through Him; and the rest is His work.

You write that your heart is often filled with sadness about the fact that you are completely feeble inwardly. It is exactly a grace to feel yourself as you are. If God wants us to feel this way, it must be pleasing to us too. Due to this we humble ourselves and acquire the ability to emerge from ourselves. Man leaves himself behind voluntarily only after he/ has realized deeply that all sanctification and salvation is only in God. But remember that you shouldn't get too much "stuck" in peering at yourself. May God grant me that at the hour of my death I do not look at myself! My spirit at times calls out from my fallen state and infirmities surrounding it: "Oh, how great and how sweet is the Lord!"(Ps. 33:9) and then I long to forget myself and to gaze at Him alone. Your letter is stamped with the image of the serpent of Moses (Numbers 21:9; John 3:14); so, avert your gaze from yourself and turn it to Jesus as this brings salvation and life.

I greet you cordially, dear sister, in sincere love in the Lord.

Thanksgiving and praise and glory to God, that He let His children communicate in the spirit, even if they never see each other in person, but I firmly believe that this will happen in heaven. Here, on earth, their unity in spirit and love in the Lord sustains them and helps them; let the Lord bless this! Lord! I commit myself to your prayers. May Jesus alone live in our hearts now and forever. Amen!

Müllheim, 4th December 1735

LETTER 107. ABOUT THE SPECIAL MERCY OF GOD, WHEN HE
LETS US SEE WHAT WE REALLY ARE. HOW SHOULD WE SEE THIS

Beloved brother!

I found your last letter dated the 22nd-29th of the past month
much more to my liking than your previous letters, because
I could understand your condition from it better than from
those. Indeed, you've been trying to write simply; but it was
not a genuine simplicity, because there was no simplicity in
you. Now you write frankly, as it is, and so let it be this way
also in future. This will give me more opportunity to help
you. It is not that I deliberately left your previous letters unanswered; I just could not. And even if it were indeed so, it's
because I don't consider myself a person who should give
advice, and NOT at all (as you write) that I consider what is
happening to you as trifles. Anyway, I don't think that I should
have written to you earlier than today.
When I see how God treats your soul, then I have no doubt
that His intention is to make something good of you. Prepare
yourself to receive this; sacrifice a lot, better to say: everything - to everyone, go for it, for everything that is required,
to follow God Who calls you truly. This is God's special grace
when He makes you feel what you really are. This self-knowledge will gradually prepare you for self-renunciation (Mark
8:34) and true conversion to God, Who alone will be our life
(Ex. 34:14).
Your soul's feelings are receptive, volatile and tender; if they
do not receive their nourishment in that what is created, then
they seek it in the spiritual domain and willingly appropriate
God and His gifts. Since the Lord, taking care of you, does not
allow your sensuality to carouse at full swing, then our fallen

nature gets angry and gnaws at anything like a dog. While your deep-seated self-love turns into cowardice.

So what are you to do? Only follow God and His saving guidance. He wants to destroy your pride and make you capable of loving Him with direct aspiration of your heart, while pride is [so to say] a crooked aiming of your love towards yourself. The Lord has inserted in you the desire to belong wholly and eternally to God. This attraction towards God lies in the very depths of the heart, in a kind of obscurity, which is impossible to grasp; while you want to transfer it to the realm of spiritual feelings and get high from it. But by turning it outward, you thereby weaken it. Let everything in your being go as it goes; be patient with yourself, also with the aridity of your soul and sensuality, without upsetting yourself and without much scrutiny, but believing that such patience pleases God (Luke 21:19). And the Lord will soon visit you and show you exactly how you should love Him and cling to Him: not by sensuality, but by faith in your heart. Then the aforementioned secret, innermost, pure attraction to God will expand, surge in you and boldly reach God (Eph. 3:12) to embrace Him and immerse in Him, and all this rather through God's than your actions. So, endure what emerges in your nature and feelings at the present moment, trying as often as possible to focus your attention on the presence of God in you. Try then in a childlike, innocent manner, as far as you are capable of and your reason tells you, to follow this presence with the help of the aforementioned attention. Don't be afraid when your ego will suddenly become active and seize your soul. In exactly same manner it will release you from its grip if you don't pay attention to it and don't allow it to confuse you. The things you write about your prayer practice, sound good. Keep an eye on two things in your practice: first, try heartily to offer good and true service to God (Neh.12:45); secondly, do not think and do not "get stuck" on how well you do it. Keep good order in the things around you: that is avoid, on the one hand, fuss, and on the other hand, indolence. Speak little. Let it be all the same to you through whom God admonishes and corrects you. Your self-love will attack you; do not despair, but take courage amongst all your infirmities. Your inner eye should be always focused on God, in whom is all our blessedness, salvation and peace. Dying to the old Adam is a seed, from which inner prayer is born and grows. Resort to the name of Jesus! May He bless your soul. In hope on Him, I remain your feeble brother.

P.S. Cordial greetings to your wife. Let the God-Infant Jesus be her treasure and joy in the new year too! I entrust her soul to the Lord; because He loves her, He will enlighten her, and may she receive this as nothing but love.

Greetings to all your friends, who love and seek the Lord!

Müllheim, 5th January 1737

Dear sister!

If the Lord arranged it that my words benefited you, remember that anything good comes from the Father of lights (James 1:17) and that we should listen only to Him. Therefore accept no gift either from me or from anyone else, if it does not lead you to God and does not nourish and pacify your heart (and this is not your feelings or reason). However, I think I understand your calling. The Lord wants you to be wholly His, and guides you on the path of the inner life, in order to unite with your spirit and detach you from being in the created and in yourself. This is the great mercy of God! Follow like a child the attraction in your heart to abide in the presence of God; just know that you must find this attraction in yourself, but not dream it.

Love the Lord and follow Him in simplicity without going into scrupulous reflections about yourself, so that your path would be free from pride. We must strive not to greatness, but to humility (Matt. 18:14), but at the same time to love God as the perfect one. The humility I'm talking about is not faint-heartedness at all, but a kind of sweetest diminishing of oneself, which is the most reliable and shortest way to the highest state of union with God (Luke 14:11).

We ought to be truly satisfied with what God gives us (or does not give), not looking for anything else and not asserting ourselves in any pursuit or activity[11] other than God Himself.

____

11 By "pursuit" and "activity" here are meant deeds of piety and ascetic deeds.

Light or darkness, enjoying grace or the soul's aridity, let everything be equally good for us when it comes from the Lord. We ourselves must neither take on anything beyond our usual responsibilities nor loosen our way of life, but surrender ourselves to the action of God at the given moment, without thinking too much about spiritual heights or lowlands. Only acting in this way we will please our God (Prov. 8:31) and rejoice in Him.

To Him, to our most precious Emmanuel, I entrust with all my heart you and your husband.

IX. On the Church and Church Life

Letter 110. On an impartial attitude to all church communities

Dear friend!

I did not reply to your previous letter, and at first I intended to do the same now. By no means because of arrogant disrespect for you, but because not in the least can I see what benefit, edification and growth in grace we can get from the discussion of the matters that you raised.

Judge for yourself: the fact whether you know my opinion about certain church communities, separatism[12] or, as you call it, sectarianism, etc. or not, cannot heal your soul or mine. More to it, whether we adhere to the same or opposite views, brings us not a hair's breadth closer to our sanctification and salvation. Moreover, due to lack of time and bodily infirmity I am forced to leave unanswered many letters that deal with much more important matters.

But then I understood from your last letter that though you do not know at all about my way of life and my way of thinking, you reproach me, without any foundation, that I allegedly sympathize with the sectarians, indulge them and so on. Therefore I consider it necessary to explain to you, dear friend, in a few words what is my attitude towards this. (However, I

12 Church separatism, unlike a schism, is not the creation of another, "parallel" Church. While belonging formally to the dominant Church, separatists do not participate in parish life. Separatists can be called only conscious Christians, who wish to pursue more or less rigorous Christian way of life, without linking themselves to the official Church rules and rites. The baptized people, who however are indifferent to the religion and do not attend the church services, cannot be called separatists. Separatists -protestants resolutely avoided attending worship services, arranging praying and preaching and meetings at home.

have spoken and written more than once; see § 20–29 in my preface to "Selected Biographies of Holy Souls"[13], etc.).

So, I believe that in the eyes of God there are, in fact, only two communities on earth, namely: the children of this world, in whom the love of a fallen world reigns (1 John 2:15), and the children of God (1 John 3:2), in whom the love of God has been poured out by the Holy Spirit (Rom. 5:5), and that God does not look at any other differences between people besides this one.

I believe (and may God make me wrong!) that in all church communities, the vast majority of pastors and the flock belong to the church of this world and of Antichrist[14] - although God keeps also among them His faithful children (Rom. 11:4). I love heartily each and every one of them.

Further. I am sure, and do not doubt it, that as well amongst the Roman Catholics as amongst Lutherans, Reformed Church, Mennonites etc. (with all the particular opinions and customs of those confessions), separatists, the souls can reach the highest peaks of sanctification and union with God

---

13 Tersteegen, Gerhard. Auserlesene Lebensbeschreibungen Heiliger Seelen... Essen, 1784. Band 1. S. XIII–XVIII.

14 "The Church of the Antichrist"; "The Church is the Whore of Babylon" (or simply "Babylon) - widespread naming of the earthly church that apostatized from Christ in the Protestant environment. Originally (in the times of Luther) they scolded in this manner the Roman Catholic Church; then the radical pietists and separatists, not to mention sectarians, began to refer these names to any church community with which those near-church groups diverged in their views. The use of these expressions is not typical for Tersteegen at all; therefore, he refers to one of the accusatory passages of his addressee.

and become worthy of entering the Church of the first-born (Heb. 12:23).

However, I believe that if a Christian, who belongs to any church community, is convinced by his conscience that certain customs adopted in this particular community go against God and obstruct the sanctification of his soul, then he must avoid participating in them. Participation would be sinful for him, "for all that is not of faith is sin." (Rom. 14:23).

Similarly, if a Christian knows for sure in his conscience that the Lord commands him to observe these customs, or that observing them or other church rules he pleases God, then he is equally bound, just as in the previous case, to follow his inner conviction and make use of this. And if any separatist would condemn such a Christian rooted in his church community, and demand that he separates from it, then such a separatist is no longer an impartial "quiet in the land"[15], but a real sectarian.

---

15 "quiet in the land", "Stillen im Lande" (Ps. 34:20,KJV) - members of different churches who turned to Christ deeper than others, but also more individualistically. For them in the first place was personal growth in Christ, above the measure of participation in church life. They avoided disputes on church dogmas and canons and strove to lead their life in stillness (Stille), detachment from the spirit of this world, prayer and surrender of oneself to God. From the outside they tried not to stand out by any peculiarities of behaviour, conscientiously performing their civic, family and household duties. They did not constitute any "parallel" church structure, but either each went to his own church, or (for the most part) abandoned formal church life.

The " quiet in the land" gathered in groups at their homes for prayer, spiritual reading and mutual edification. Once or twice a week, large gatherings were held for preaching and prayer. In fact it was "moderate" church separatism, which took shape in the environment of the Lower Rhine Reformed Pietism. The "quiet in the land" differed from real separatism in that the question of participation (or degree of participation) in church life was left to the personal choice of each " quiet in the land" one. Gerhard Tersteegen, who was spiritually educated in the traditions of " quiet in the land" was the most significant

As for me and my way of life: I don't condemn or scold any church community, as sectarians do; neither I am a separatist, since I have not separated from my church and I'm not going to do so. However, I don't go to any church for worship[16], because my conscience prevents it.

16 Lit.: zum Abendmahl, for the Lord's Supper. For an Orthodox reader Tersteegen's refusal to participate in the Sacrament of Communion (however not a complete refusal; in his early years he took communion, at least during his confirmation) seems to be a grave temptation and, so to speak, "casts a shadow" on everything he wrote.

But it is necessary for an Orthodox reader to take into account the following four important specifics:

1) A significant difference in the perception of this Sacrament between the Orthodox (and Catholic) and Reformed Churches. For Orthodox (and Catholics) communion of the Holy Mysteries of Christ is an indispensable and central source of the spiritual life, both personal and communal. The Reformed attach less significance to the sacrament of Communion. The Sacrament of the Supper is not perceived as the centre of spiritual and church life; it is done not at every Sunday service. The core of the worship is the gathering together of the community, joint prayer and sermon, while communion is a kind of addition. For the Reformed, usually communion seldom takes place.

2) In the Reformed Church, as opposed to the Catholic and Orthodox Churches, there is no confession, which also performs the function of "admission" to communion. Therefore, when the Sacrament is performed, everyone joins in, whoever wants to, including unrepentant sinners. Tersteegen, as could be seen from several of his treatises on communion (see: Gerhard Tersteegen's Nachgelassene Aufsatze und Abhandlungen. Essen, 1842. S. 1–77), treated this Sacrament gravely and with great reverence; so for him it was morally and spiritually unacceptable to take communion from one Chalice and thus testify to his unity in Christ with, say, an usurer or madam of a brothel, and in general with people for whom Christ and the Church are not the centre of life, but just a custom.

I see no reason why I should follow again this custom. However, if I would become confident that God would be glorified more through my participation in the divine worship than through non-participation, and that I and my neighbors would truly benefit from it and grow in God, then I would not persist in my current opinion.

3) Perhaps the most important: the Reformed believe that the efficacy of the Sacrament depends on the spiritual and moral dignity of the communicant. Thereby it loses its objective significance, which puts the community into a situation where "profanation" of communion may occur (that is, if in a church meeting, the Sacrament is invalid for one communicant, this invalidity might affect other participants too). To avoid this, one has to avoid communion with persons about whose state nothing is known, not to mention obvious sinners.

Of course, in such an approach, from the Orthodox point of view, there is a certain "overshoot", an obvious rigorism; but at least it is perfectly understandable and largely justified.

4) Tersteegen was a man who held fast to his traditions. He accepted Christianity consciously, in his youth, in the environment of Reformed Pietism and separatism, the centre of which for many decades was Müllheim an der Ruhr.

This environment was characterized precisely by the above-described rigoristic approach to communion. One of the "pillars" of this tendency, Hochmans von Hochenau (1670–1721), wrote: "With regard to the Holy Communion, I believe that it is established only for the chosen disciples of Christ who will follow Christ in deed and in truth, rejecting every spirit of this world. Therefore, the Covenant of God is devalued, and His wrath is aroused on the whole Church, when the wicked children of this world are admitted to the Lord's Supper, which, alas, is happening even now" (Ernst Christoph Hochmans von Hochenau Glaubensbekenntnis: Geschrieben aus seinem Arrest... [S. l.], 1709. S. 5). Tersteegen therefore has adopted this view. However, unlike his more radical teachers and contemporaries, he never made these rigorous demands on others, but referred them only to himself.

When I have the opportunity to hear a good preacher of the Reformed, Lutherans, etc., then I go to church to listen to his sermon; and if the Catholics would have had such a preacher (as I knew some in the past), then without any embarrassment I would go to hear him too. However, of course with the exception of those cases when this freedom of mine could be a temptation to the weak (1 Cor. 8:9).

And as in every nation he who fears the Lord and who works justice is acceptable to Him (Acts 10:35), so is he acceptable to me, whatever church he belongs to. In fact I have fellowship with representatives of all church communities. I speak to them when God gives this, both publicly and privately about the grace of God in Christ, about self-renunciation, about love for God, about prayer, without going into peculiarities and different opinions of those churches to which my interlocutors belong and which God Himself has determined and allowed to exist on earth (Acts 5:38-39).

Abstract questions and differences of opinion in the church communities are of little interest to me (or of no interest at all); I can say the same about the favorite and widely proclaimed views of many separatists[17], such as about the date of the coming of the Antichrist, about a thousand-years kingdom, about repentance after death, about the restoration of everything, etc. To become dead with regard to myself and to the entire fallen creation in order to come to love God in Jesus Christ – this is the only secret of my faith. With regard to other matters I am stupid and I hope to become even more stupid in this regard.

To put it briefly: I am by no means an over-thrower of the material Babylon[18], but I'm only seeking how to destroy, with

---

17 More precisely, all pietists in general (especially radical ones); these questions were their favourite topics.

18 See note 7.

the help of the grace of God, the Babylon in my heart (and in the hearts of others) and to set up there the Kingdom of God instead, which "is not food and drink, but rather justice and peace and joy, in the Holy Spirit". (Rom. 14:17).

Here you are, dear friend, I've clearly enough (as I think) set out my views to you and I will be glad if these explanations would satisfy you.

If your thoughts are different from mine, don't worry about it. Our knowledge on earth is always partial, divinatory (1 Cor. 13:9, 12); when we will be home, in heaven (2 Cor. 5:1), then from there we will see everything as it is.

If you disagree with me, please do not write to me about that, for I have neither the time nor the inclination to upset myself in disputes. Let 's better ourselves, forgetting those things that are behind, and extending ourselves toward those things that are ahead, to pursue the destination, the prize of the heavenly calling of God in Christ Jesus. (Philippians 3:14)."

I will tell you in conclusion one more thing, beloved friend in the Lord, accept this word of truth and sincere love: that your zeal against Babylon or against the so-called sectarian does not come from the spirit of Christ, but mostly from your own, natural fire kindled by your sorrow with regard to the miserable condition of the Church. This fire burns you, while not in the least the foundations of Babylon. You need, just like I, not this fire, but a constant ardent hunger and thirst for grace and love of Christ. Your communion with this meek love will soften the harsh aspirations of the fallen nature, and then you will be able to look at your poor neighbors with a kind eye, carry their burdens (Gal. 6:2) and love them. Otherwise, dear friend, you will regret very much at the end of your days that you used your best powers, zeal and time for useless things. May God give you and me in this and in everything else wisdom and grace. Striving to abide in Him, I remain your cordially devoted friend.

Müllheim, 9th March 1735

LETTER 111. ON THE CHURCH SERVICE

Beloved friend and brother in Christ!

May the Lord Jesus speak peace to your soul!
I cannot leave unanswered your last letter from November
16, for I am not at all indifferent with regard to the prosperity
and peace of your soul. But since no one may rule over the
conscience of another person, then do not expect from me
anything but humble reflections on the matters which em-
barrass you. These reflections in no way oblige you to accept
them or follow them, unless when your soul receives a notice
from the Lord to consent to them.
In no case do I want to reject, nor, moreover, humiliate the
church service. On the contrary, I think that there is much
good in it. The church worship, when used in moderation and
in a proper way, pleases God and brings us great benefits.
However church worship brings this benefit not by itself, but
in accordance with its disposition towards inner worship: either as a means which leads to inner worship, or as the manifestation of inner worship and its fruit. On this earth the spirit does all the good through the body. It is in this, and not in
any other sense that the Lord Jesus gave us some rules. These
rules are however not an indispensable law which we must
observe for the sake of having a clear conscience.
It is highly reprehensible when one Christian troubles or saddens another Christian because of something purely external.
More to it, one should not do so in relation to oneself. Our justification and reconciliation with God is only and solely Jesus
Christ Himself. When we undertake or abandon something
external, it should be done in the Lord, in faith, that thereby
His good will is done. But at the same time with child-like
freedom, so as neither to rely on what is done, nor to worry

about what is left behind; "For the kingdom of God is not food and drink, but rather justice and peace and joy, in the Holy Spirit. For he who serves Christ in this, pleases God and is proven before men." (Rom. 14:17-18). By adhering to this, we can be completely at peace in our conscience.

Having stated these principles, I must draw your attention to the fact that the commands and prohibitions, commanded to us in Scripture, must be considered and carried out not all in the same way. Prohibitions are completely certain and allow no exceptions. Decrees as far as they relate to the external actions, are not quite the same, since the following addendum must always be attached to them: if there are appropriate capabilities for this. For example: stealing, revenge, slander, etc. is absolutely prohibited; we should never do this and under no circumstances. However fasting, giving alms, giving shelter to strangers and many more of this kind, are the commandments which man in his particular circumstances, may not always be able to perform. In such cases it will not be imputed to him as a transgression. Church rules must be seen similarly: their non-observance in cases when we do not have the means or the possibility to observe them according to God's will and in God's Spirit should burden our conscience just as little (if not less), as the above mentioned non-observance of some commandments.

If I had not been baptized, then I would let myself be baptized, but not because that baptism in itself[19] justifies me or reconciles me with God, because it can't, but out of obedience and reverence for the commandment of the Lord Jesus Christ (Matthew 28:19; Acts 10:48 and many others). If it were not

19 The Protestant understanding of the sacraments comes from the conviction that they are secondary in relation to faith (Mark 16:16). Sacraments seal (Baptism) or reinforce (Communion) faith, but in themselves, without faith, they are meaningless. See note. 1 to letter 112.

for the last one, I might not let myself have been baptized e.g. there, where I would be forced to accept that my salvation depends solely on the observing of one or another rule. For I believe that if it were not an opportunity in my life to be baptized properly, then this fact still wouldn't be an obstacle to obtaining unity with the Lord and a honorable death in Him[20]. However when I may confess the aforementioned freely, I would gladly be baptized, even in the most outwardly solemn manner, so to testify that I belong to my Lord.

In the same way do I reason about the Sacrament of the Altar and about the gathering of the faithful. I am willing, with the freedom of a Christian, to receive communion and attend liturgical worship, if I have a good opportunity for this. But since, unlike Baptism (performed only once and personally) the Sacrament of the Altar is constantly repeated and always binds us to other people, then large difficulties arise. The worship and the sacrament are currently arranged in such a way that it is impossible to be in the gathering and partake of the Sacrament without entering into unity not only with pious Christians (of whom there are always and everywhere few), but also with an overwhelming majority of Christians-in-name, who actually live "in accordance to the influences of the world, and not in accordance with Christ" (Col. 2:8). And this can prevent us in the pursuit of our destination[21](Philippians 3:14) and gives reason to think whether it would not be better for us to stop attending such services rather than partaking in them not in God's spirit. I'm not talking about

---

20 In the history of the Church of the first three centuries, we see many martyrs, who were not baptized and yet canonized as saints for their martyrdom.

21 On the peculiarities of the understanding of the sacrament in the Reformed Church, see note 5 to letter 110.

another evil that comes from here, namely, that the zealots of piety undertake to seek "especially pure" communities for themselves and join them. However all such communities do not in the least avoid all kinds of confusion of truth and falsehood. As a result of this, even though they do not want it, they become, without realizing this, of "two minds" (James 1:8) and stop loving their brothers and sisters, who do not belong to their community. We see numerous sad examples of this even at those who began with the Spirit (Gal. 3:3). Therefore, Christians who belong to one or another church, should remain there (1 Cor. 7:24), and seek nourishment for the soul and peace of conscience under their own conditions. God is not bound by any place or community and He has those who are His everywhere (Rom. 11:4).

As for the communion itself, it was established by the Lord Jesus in simplicity, for holy strengthening and renewal of love for Him and for one another. The essence of this Mystery is that He shares Himself with us, while we partake and share ourselves with each other, in all respects; not by chance did the first Christians have everything in common (Acts 2:44; 4:32). They had common meals at their homes, after the meal breaking bread in love (Acts 2:46), without any bylaw and solemn ceremonies. I don't know whether there is on earth any church which retains their initial simplicity and freedom. The Lord's Supper has become long since a command, duty, the cause of separation, while it should be the only Meal of Love. I do not condemn at all the changes that people have brought in it in the course of time. Times and people change, and the church customs change with them, and God accepts this, but only if all the rules and rites contribute to love and godliness and are used in a good and righteous disposition of the heart. The Lord Jesus, by establishing this Sacrament, did not want to burden, but to strengthen us without imposing a yoke of a new law upon our conscience and spiritual freedom. Otherwise, it would be necessary to impose a law of foot washing for all Christians, since Christ ordered this with more stress than the breaking of bread and drinking wine in His commemoration (John 13:14). This however is not observed in any Christian Church.

The Lord did not say anything about the frequency of the gathering of Christians and with how many they should be. He did not say a word about ranks and rites.

I wonder what might get in the way of the home worship of the faithful? The two or three is already the gathering, in the midst of which Christ Himself promised to be present (Matthew 18:20). Husband and wife which are united in their following the Lord, who love Him, who love one another before Him: is not their house a real church? Spouses together with their like-minded friends, who are just as heartily striving to the Lord: are they not the true assembly of faithful, even if during this meeting not many prayers and edifying words are pronounced? I assure you that I, with an incomparably greater desire would attend such a worship, than some thousand-strong church festival.

And if two or three are gathered in His name (Matt. 18:20), with a pure disposition and good intention, edifying one another in the love of the Lord (1 Thessalonians 5:11) and desiring communion and partaking in Jesus and being for one another one heart and one soul (Acts 4:32), should have a meal together22, would it not also be the supper of Christ, pleasing to God by no means less than the most solemn mass in the most beautiful church (despite the fact that I do not at all undermine the value of the latter)? Carry out this service,

---

22 The author doesn't mean "breaking bread" (Brotbrechen), as in Acts. 2: 20, that is the Eucharist; that is, not about the celebration of the Sacrament under the home Conditions. Tersteegen never did this and prompted no one else to do so, considering such a home breaking bread as a sign of sectarianism. By this home meal he meant "agape", joint meal of love (Zusammenessen)

my friend, as often as possible, and I will be joyfully attending it in the spirit!

Generally speaking, one should never forget that one is not justified by the works of the law, but only by faith in Jesus Christ (Gal. 2:16; Phil. 3:9). It is good to use rules and rites as a means and in accordance with one's personal circumstances, paying tribute to the church worship. However it is good only when we understand that such worship cannot make its participant perfect as concerns his conscience(Heb. 9:9). Yes, even one's complete obedience to one's conscience (which is, however, necessary in every possible way) will not lead one to its indestructible tranquility and to peace with God. Even if a soul, with all its sincerity and zeal will accomplish everything it is capable of, the end of this will be as the Apostle Paul writes in his Epistle to the Romans: "Unhappy man that I am, who will free me from this body of death?" (Rom. 7:24).

Deliverance from all pangs of conscience occurs only when the soul, having become fully aware of its impotence, immerses itself in humility and poverty of spirit and then comes out of itself and by the means of its innermost faith merges with the Lord Jesus Christ. Then He will become the end of the law (Rom. 10:4) for the soul. For "there is now no condemnation for those who are in Christ Jesus, who are not walking according to the flesh." (Rom. 8:1). And this is the real foundation and the true beginning of the true inner Christian life. And the soul which is called to such a life in the spirit (Rom. 8:1) and sees the beginnings of this inner life inside itself, should dedicate itself faithfully and solely to this and follow God's vocation. Such a soul mustn't attempt to return under the yoke of the law; because now it lives in the grace and under "the law of the Spirit of life in Christ Jesus (Rom. 8:2)." It should not return under guidance of its troubled and full of doubts conscience either, which conscience hopes to appease itself by some external or its ego's action. From now on the soul cherishes and receives all its righteousness, rest and peace from the innermost faith in Jesus and abiding in Him. Please pay attention to this!

Usually when a soul which lives an inner life, would be overwhelmed by darkness, narrowness, impoverishment, sorrows, distraction and therefore upset, and because of that can't find back its own place, and things aren't going the way they usually do, and from this it becomes even more embarrassed and confused, then the soul begins to investigate intensely what could be the reasons of this, but in vain. Here the soul must not seek and not rush about, but having generally confessed its infidelity, come to terms with this and having lost itself, cling again to Christ (Matthew 16:25). If the soul does not do this and continues to wallow in itself, then it will again fall under the restless supervision of its conscience and will try all kinds of actions, thinking to help itself with one or another self-willed feat; participation in one or another church rite or observing one or another church rule; but it is all in vain. The soul will find durable and unshakable rest and peace only, as I have already said, when it once again immerses itself in Jesus, Who alone will fulfill all the law in it (Rom. 10:4). The only thing the soul must do is to endure its sorrows patiently and with a humble hope on Him. Then, owing to such a meek awaiting of the promises of God, quietly immersing itself in the Lord and peacefully enduring sorrows, the soul gradually returns to its place and finds peace with God through our Lord Jesus Christ (Rom. 5:1). Having no understanding of this many pious souls make mistakes, get trapped in them and thereby inflict senseless suffering on themselves. So, may it be our main concern to stay by true faith in Jesus and become rooted in Him, so that He becomes our life and our peace (Col. 3:4; Eph. 2:14). Then we, living in the spirit, will bear the true fruits of the spirit, listed in the

Letter to the Galatians. There is no law against those fruits. (Gal. 5:22-25).
I was thinking of writing you a few lines in reply, but it turned out to be such a big message, and quite confusing because of my troubled head. Take in love what suits you; I will be happy if you learn from it something instructive or useful for yourself.

I greet you and your lovely wife in the Lord; May He bless you both. I remain, by grace, your loving brother and friend.

Müllheim, 18th December 1736